THE PERCEPTUAL SHIFT

The Perceptual Shift

*How to Love Your Life
and Manifest Abundance*

JAMES QUINE

The Gecko Group

THE PERCEPTUAL SHIFT

The Gecko Group

THE PERCEPTUAL SHIFT, Copyright © 2024 by James Quine
All rights reserved. Printed in the United States of America.
No part of this book may be used or reproduced in any manner
whatsoever without written permission except in the case of
brief quotations embodied in critical articles and reviews.
For information, address The Gecko Group,
5095 Napilihau St, 109B-385, Lahaina, HI 96761.

The Gecko Group books may be purchased for educational, business,
or sales promotional use. For information, please email the
Special Markets Department at GGsales@gmail.com.

Gecko Group hardcover published 2025.

FIRST EDITION

Designed by James Quine

ACKNOWLEDGMENTS

I want to take a moment to express my heartfelt gratitude to the individuals and communities that have encouraged, inspired, and supported me throughout the journey of writing this book.

The love and support of my family and friends have been invaluable—your wisdom, love, and presence in my life are priceless gifts that continue to shape and sustain me. A special thanks to my older brother, Robert, who has stood by my side through life's ups and downs, offering thoughtful edits, humility, and a kind sense of humor; to my eldest son, who helped with the cover design; and to my youngest daughter—whose editorial guidance was instrumental in shaping this book—thank you for always believing in me. I am deeply grateful to you both, and to my other children, whose unique light and love continue to inspire me every day.

I also want to honor the many communities that have helped me grow—especially those rooted in deep reflection, spiritual connection, and mutual support. These sacred circles of healing have offered me clarity, humility, and connection over many decades, and I remain deeply grateful for the ways they've changed my life.

I extend my thanks to the authors and teachers who have profoundly influenced my perspective. Deepak Chopra introduced me to the transformative power of meditation, while Oprah Winfrey's optimism and philanthropic spirit have inspired me to embrace a life of purpose and generosity. I am also indebted to the wisdom of Melody Beattie, Iyanla Vanzant, Eckhart Tolle, Paul O., M.J. Ryan, Ryan Holiday, and Alan Cohen, whose works have been a daily source of inspiration for decades.

Finally, I want to honor the universal energy that sustains and inspires all life. This profound connection motivates me each day to become my best self and contribute positively to the world.

To this source of life and love, I offer my deepest gratitude.

ABOUT THE AUTHOR

My own journey to this place has been anything but linear...

Raised in Hollywood and Beverly Hills in the entertainment industry, my early life was chaos—expulsions, addiction, and running away. By my late teens, I was living on the streets of Los Angeles, trapped in cycles of self-destruction, reacting to life instead of responding to it. As a teenager, I tried to end my life—once by slitting my wrists, another time by attempting to drive off a cliff. Both times, I failed. My parents truly did their best.

Interventions—boarding school, foster care, and therapy—offered lifelines. A counselor's words and my father's sobriety led me to a turning point: on January 14, 1982, I gave up drugs and alcohol. With a clearer mind and renewed focus, I attended community college, then USC, and built a career in real estate, publishing, and entrepreneurship. I married, became a parent, and eventually made a home for my family on the island of Maui.

Yet pain lingered, and once again, I attempted suicide—this time by trying to jump from atop a parking structure in Santa Monica. That, too, failed.

Through deep self-work, a shift in perception, and help from others, I learned to embrace abundance and love my life—no matter what. Then life tested me again. I was diagnosed with an inoperable brain tumor and given three weeks to live. But something remarkable happened—the tumor began to shrink, and within two years, it had disappeared. Did my mindset play a role in my recovery? I can't prove it, but I believe it did.

This book is based on what I've learned over 63 years of living, but I am still a work in progress. I make mistakes. Sometimes I hurt people I love. But I've learned to make amends, keep trying, and be gentle with myself.

My hope is that these pages give you the same hope I've found—a lifeline back to happiness. That they help you see life through a new lens, revealing the beauty, abundance, and joy that have always been there. And if this book helps even one person, I'll be grateful to have made a difference.

Your abundant life awaits you...

INTRODUCTION

Welcome to this transformative experience in *Perceptual Shifting*. This book is designed to help you see life through a new lens—one that focuses on gratitude, optimism, and abundance. It's a roadmap for turning challenges into opportunities, finding joy in everyday moments, and creating a life beyond your wildest dreams.

Whether you're here to improve your relationships, deepen your personal growth, manifest your deepest desires, or simply learn to love your life, this book provides tools and practices to help you achieve these goals. For those unsure about the difference between **perception** and **perspective**:

- **Perception** is how you interpret the world around you.
- **Perspective** is the viewpoint or lens through which you see and make sense of it.

Here's a simple exercise to illustrate this concept: Raise your arm and point your index finger toward the sky. Now look up at it and rotate your hand in a clockwise direction, keeping an eye on it. Continuing the rotation, slowly lower your hand to chest level, and then to your waist while maintaining the motion. Looking down, which way does it appear to be moving?

The direction your hand appears to move depends on your **perspective**, while your **perception** is how you interpret it. Your hand's movement hasn't changed—by shifting your perspective, your perception shifted.

This simple exercise demonstrates the powerful connection between **perception** and **perspective**. Throughout this book, you'll find tools and practices to help you **intentionally shift your perception**, empowering you to experience profound happiness and abundance in every aspect of life.

CONTENTS

PART I: AWAKENING YOUR AWARENESS	**1**

The Lens Through Which We See 3
How your perceptions shape reality.

The Roots of Our Perceptions 13
Reevaluating inherited beliefs.

PART II: EMBRACING THE SHIFT	**25**

The Power of Mindset Shifting 27
Expanding your awareness.

The Art of Reframing 39
From challenges to opportunities.

Transforming Through Transitions 57
Embracing the change.

Gratitude as a Compass 73
The journey toward abundance.

Perceptual Shifting in Relationships 87
Playing well with others.

PART III: MANIFESTING ABUNDANCE — 111

Reinventing Your Roadmap — 113
Reshape your future.

Living in The Perceptual Shift — 135
Cultivating a habit of love.

Envisioning Your Abundant Life — 157
Finding the buried treasures.

Abundance Manifestation Practices — 181
Turning dreams into reality.

Living in the Perceptual Shift — 223
The road to transformation.

A Final Reflection — 239
Closing thoughts from the author.

Daily Practices of Life Lovers — 241
Essential routines to foster abundance.

Resources to Expand Your Journey — 245
Recommended reading.

Creating a Circle of Love — 247
Support and service.

AWAKENING YOUR AWARENESS

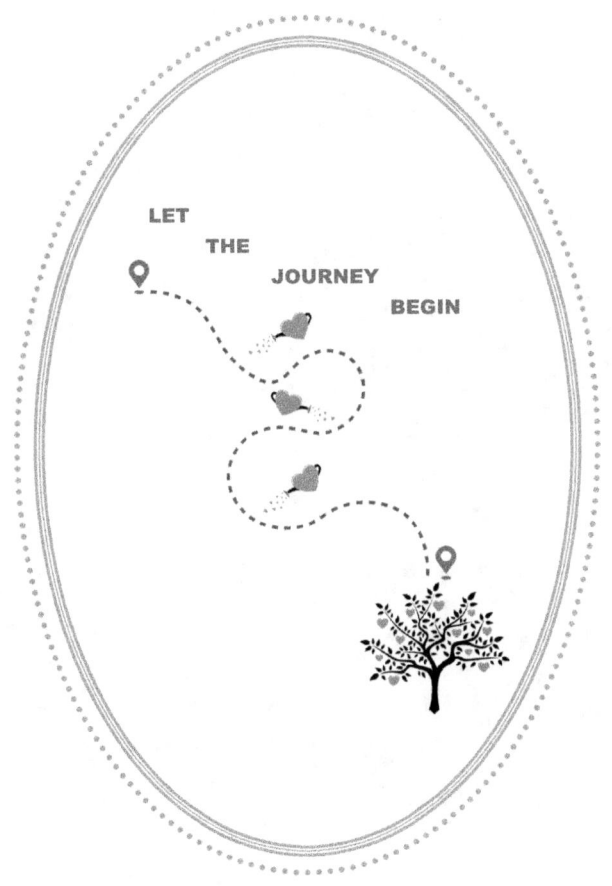

The Lens Through Which We See

HOW YOUR PERCEPTIONS SHAPE REALITY

Imagine standing atop a hill on a clear day. Below, the landscape stretches endlessly, with rivers winding through valleys and roads crisscrossing the land. Now picture yourself looking through a pair of tinted glasses. Depending on the color of the tint, the view might appear golden, somber, or even distorted.

This metaphor illustrates the essence of perception: the lens through which we view the world profoundly affects how we experience it.

Perception is more than just seeing; it's the process by which we interpret and assign meaning to everything around us. It influences our emotions, shapes our decisions, and ultimately defines our reality. This chapter explores the science and psychology behind perception, demonstrating how it impacts every facet of life—from the mundane to the extraordinary.

Are you willing to commit to seeing this book through—fully engaging in the exercises—to polish the lens you see life through, inviting more abundance, deeper connections, and a greater sense of peace? _____

If so, list five gifts you would like to manifest by doing so—whether it's love, financial freedom, creativity, confidence, or anything else your heart desires.

_____

_____

_____

_____

_____

THE SCIENCE OF PERCEPTION: HOW IT WORKS

At its core, perception is a neurological process. When you see, hear, or touch something, your brain receives input from sensory organs and processes this information to form an understanding of your environment. However, this process is not purely objective. While the raw data—light waves, sound vibrations, or tactile sensations—remains consistent, the interpretation of this data varies widely among individuals.

For instance, two people might hear the same piece of music. One person may feel elation, recalling joyous memories, while the other may feel sadness due to a melancholic association. This contrast arises because perception is influenced by past experiences, beliefs, emotions, and even biological factors like age or health.

Neuroscientists have discovered that perception involves not only the sensory areas of the brain but also higher-order cognitive functions. The prefrontal cortex, responsible for decision-making and problem-solving, plays a crucial role in shaping how we perceive sensory input and assign meaning to it. This means that perception is not a passive process; it is active and dynamic, constantly influenced by our internal states and external environments.

Have you ever had a conversation where both you and the other person believed you were right—and it led to hurt feelings? _____

If so, write down the situation and reflect on how seeing it from their perspective could have created a better interaction.

_____

_____

_____

_____

FILTERS OF THE MIND

Psychologists have long studied how perception influences behavior and decision-making. One foundational concept is the idea of cognitive biases—habits of thinking that lead us to stray from clear, logical decision-making. These biases act as mental shortcuts, helping us navigate a complex world but often distorting our perception of reality.

For example, confirmation bias frequently causes individuals to favor information that aligns with their existing beliefs while completely ignoring contradictory evidence. This behavior tends to reinforce negative thought patterns and limit personal growth.

Similarly, negativity bias—our tendency to focus more on negative events than positive ones—can distort our perception of life's balance. It often makes challenges feel more overwhelming than they actually are and can even obscure the hope of a 'light at the end of the tunnel.'

Another key concept is the "self-fulfilling prophecy." If you perceive yourself as incapable or unworthy, your actions will likely align with that belief, leading to outcomes that reinforce your perception. Conversely, a positive self-view can lead to confidence, achievement, and new opportunities.

Do you ever find yourself focusing on negative events? _____

If so, write down one you've been thinking about lately and how becoming aware of the destructiveness of this type of thinking might help you see things more clearly.

_____

_____

_____

_____

_____

PERCEPTION SHAPES EMOTIONS

Consider this scenario: you're walking down the street, and a friend passes by without acknowledging you. If your perception leans toward insecurity, you might interpret their behavior as intentional avoidance, leading to feelings of hurt or anger. But if you view the situation with compassion, you might assume they were simply preoccupied or distracted—sparing yourself unnecessary emotional distress.

This example highlights how perception directly shapes our emotional responses. By consciously shifting how we interpret events, we can transform our inner emotional landscape.

Practices such as mindfulness and cognitive reframing help us pause, reflect, and examine our perceptions. They empower us to respond with greater clarity, balance, and intention—rather than reacting impulsively or falling back on outdated "fight, flight, or freeze" patterns.

Have you recently reacted in a way that didn't align with the best version of yourself? _____

If so, describe the most recent time this occurred and how a shift in perception might have changed the outcome.

_____

_____

_____

_____

_____

_____

_____

PERCEPTION DRIVES DECISIONS

Our choices are deeply influenced by how we perceive the world. For instance, someone who views life through a lens of abundance may take bold risks and embrace opportunities, trusting that there's always more to gain. In contrast, someone who sees the world as scarce may hoard resources and avoid risks, driven by a fear of loss.

Research in behavioral economics supports this idea. Daniel Kahneman and Amos Tversky's prospect theory demonstrates that people's decisions are shaped more by the perception of potential losses than by equivalent gains—often leading to irrational choices or missed opportunities.

Recognizing the role perception plays in our decision-making empowers us to pause, question automatic reactions, and make intentional choices that align with our values. Simply becoming aware of this influence can open the door to a life rooted in happiness, abundance, and inner peace—and unlock extraordinary possibilities.

Do you usually make decisions from a place of fear and scarcity rather than trust and abundance? _____

If so, where do you think that mindset came from, and are you ready to shift it so your decisions flow with the confidence that everything will work out for the best?

_____

_____

_____

_____

_____

_____

_____

PERCEPTION DEFINES OUTCOMES

On a broader scale, perception shapes the trajectory of our lives. A person who views setbacks as learning opportunities is far more likely to persevere and succeed than someone who sees them as insurmountable failures. Cultivating a positive, growth-oriented mindset fosters resilience, creativity, and overall well-being—creating the foundation for lasting change.

The powerful link between perception and outcomes is vividly illustrated by the placebo effect. When patients believe a treatment will work, that belief alone can spark real physiological changes—even when the treatment is inactive. This phenomenon underscores how perception can produce tangible, measurable results.

Perception also shapes how others respond to us. Studies show that individuals who view themselves as confident and capable are often perceived that way by others—creating a reinforcing cycle of trust, influence, and success.

This self-fulfilling feedback loop reminds us that how we see ourselves—and the world around us—directly impacts the opportunities we attract, the relationships we cultivate, and the challenges we overcome. Mastering our perception gives us the power to shape reality with clarity, intention, and purpose.

Do you believe that positively shifting your perception can create more abundance in your life? _____

If so, write down specific areas—relationships, career, health, finances—where you'd like to see more abundance.

_____

_____

_____

_____

SHIFTING PERCEPTIONS

While perception is powerful, it is not fixed. The art of *Perceptual Shifting*—the ability to consciously change how we view situations—offers a pathway to personal transformation. This process begins with awareness: recognizing when a perception is limiting or misaligned with reality. From there, intentional practices like journaling, visualization, and seeking alternative perspectives can help reframe perceptions.

For example, someone who perceives public speaking as terrifying might reframe it as an opportunity to share ideas and connect with others. Over time, this new perception can diminish fear and build confidence.

Similarly, a person who habitually blames others for their struggles might start shifting their perspective, transforming feelings of victimization into compassion. By recognizing that others are also on their own spiritual journeys—often stuck or struggling themselves—we can break free from blame, reclaim our power, and grow with compassion.

Have you ever had a negative or doubtful thought about yourself or a situation? _____

If so, write down that thought and then write the opposite of it. How might this new perspective create a better outcome?

_____

_____

_____

_____

_____

_____

THE RIPPLE EFFECT OF PERCEPTION

The impact of perception extends far beyond the individual. A single shift in perception can influence relationships, communities, and even global systems. Leaders who view challenges as opportunities inspire innovation and collaboration. Communities that perceive diversity as a strength foster inclusivity and progress.

This ripple effect underscores the collective power of *Perceptual Shifts*. By changing how we see, we contribute to a more compassionate, equitable, and abundant society while simultaneously creating a richer, more fulfilling life for ourselves.

On a more intimate level, our perceptions directly shape the way we engage with those closest to us—our family, friends, and significant others. When we choose to see the best in our loved ones, offer understanding instead of judgment, and view conflict as an opportunity for growth—not a battle to be won—our relationships naturally strengthen.

Perceptual Shifting changes how we perceive and respond to others. It can transform family dynamics, deepen romantic connections, and help heal long-standing misunderstandings. It influences the way we love—and how we're loved in return.

Do you think your family or friends would be positively affected if you felt more grateful, kind, and optimistic? _____

If so, list those people who might be most profoundly affected by your new, more abundant lifestyle.

_____

_____

_____

_____

EMBRACING THE PATH

The power of perception lies in its duality: it can either limit us or set us free. By understanding the science and psychology behind perception, we gain the tools to harness its potential. The journey of *Perceptual Shifting* is one of self-discovery, resilience, and empowerment—a journey that redefines not only how we see the world but also how we live within it.

As you delve deeper into the chapters ahead, you'll learn practical strategies to identify, challenge, and shift perceptions—unlocking new possibilities for joy, growth, and abundance. The lens through which you view life is yours to shape—and with it, the reality you create.

This is a transformative process, one that calls for commitment and sincerity. If you dedicate yourself to the work, the rewards will be profound. Clarity, inner peace, and a life rich with purpose await those who engage fully. At the same time, approach the journey with curiosity and a playful spirit. Personal growth is not about perfection—it's about progress. Take it seriously, but don't forget to savor the process.

Let's embrace this path together, with dedication and enthusiasm!

Have you ever had someone say something nice about you, but you didn't fully believe it yourself? _____

If so, write down what they said, how it felt, and how believing it about yourself might change the way you see yourself.

_____

_____

_____

_____

_____

The Roots of Our Perceptions
REEVALUATING INHERITED BELIEFS

Imagine sampling two dishes of creamy, fragrant chai tea prepared by different chefs, each proudly using their great-grandmother's cherished recipe.

The first chef, from the bustling streets of Mumbai, steeps rich black tea leaves in fresh whole milk, layering the flavors with cardamom, ginger, cinnamon, cloves, and black pepper. The result is bold and vibrant, the spices dancing energetically on your tongue, awakening your senses with warmth and intensity.

The second chef, hailing from a tranquil Himalayan village in Nepal, brews the same drink, but the spices are subtler, gently infused into the delicate sweetness of goat's milk, accented with notes of nutmeg and vanilla. Here, the flavor unfolds gradually, comforting and mild, offering warmth without overwhelming your palate.

Both chefs followed recipes handed down through generations, yet your experience tasting their chai differs profoundly. Your preference for one or the other is deeply personal, shaped by your own upbringing, cultural background, and lived experiences.

Each of us carries perceptions deeply rooted in our upbringing, culture, and personal experiences. These roots—often hidden and unexamined—shape how we interpret events, engage with others, and view ourselves.

Often, we're unaware of the assumptions and beliefs we've quietly inherited. Yet these unseen influences operate in the background, quietly shaping our choices and self-perception—sometimes even holding us back from loving our lives and manifesting abundance.

This chapter explores the origins of our perceptions: how they are formed by family, culture, and past experiences, and the ways they can either limit or empower us. By understanding the roots of these perceptions, we can begin the essential work of reshaping them to align more fully with who we truly are.

Was there someone in your past whose behaviors, words, or attitudes negatively impacted you? _____

If so, write down who this person was and describe the specific behaviors, words, or attitudes that affected you.

_____

_____

_____

Reflect on how carrying this person's influence may still impact your daily life or relationships today.

_____

_____

_____

Would letting go of their negative impact benefit you? _____

If so, write a statement declaring your intention to reclaim your power over these past experiences, shaping your own future from this point forward.

_____

_____

_____

THE INFLUENCE OF FAMILY

Our family of origin imprints early patterns that shape our worldview. From an early age, we absorb beliefs, values, and behaviors modeled by parents, siblings, and extended family. If you grew up in a household that emphasized scarcity, with sayings like *"Money doesn't grow on trees"* or *"You'll never get ahead in life,"* you may carry a deep-seated fear around money or a sense of financial insecurity—even if your current circumstances don't warrant it.

On the other hand, families that fostered a sense of possibility and resilience—*"You can achieve anything you set your mind to"*—might instill a more optimistic outlook. Yet even positive influences can bring unintentional baggage. For example, the pressure to always excel can lead to perfectionism and chronic stress.

Recognizing how family dynamics have shaped your perceptions is the first step in understanding your lens. It's not about placing blame but about identifying and understanding patterns that no longer serve you. With this awareness, you can make the necessary attitude adjustments, consciously transforming these perceptions into ones that empower you and reflect your true self.

Is there anyone in your family who has had a positive influence on you? life? _____

If so, write down who they are and how their influence has positively changed the way you see things.

_____

_____

_____

_____

CULTURAL CONDITIONING

Beyond family, culture plays a significant role in shaping our views. Societal norms, traditions, and collective beliefs act as powerful forces that influence how we see the world and our place in it.

For example, Western cultures often prioritize individualism, encouraging personal success and self-reliance. In contrast, many Eastern cultures emphasize collectivism, valuing community and harmony over individual achievement.

While cultural conditioning provides a framework for navigating life, it can also impose limiting beliefs. Messages like *"This is just the way things are"* or *"People like us don't do things like that"* can stifle creativity and ambition.

Challenging cultural narratives takes courage, but it can unlock new opportunities and foster a more authentic, expansive perspective on the world.

Have you had others speak to you in a way that made you hesitant to move forward or approach life with optimism? _____

If so, write down who it was, what they said that made you feel limited or doubtful, and how the opposite message could create a **Perceptual Shift**.

_____

_____

_____

_____

_____

_____

THE WEIGHT OF OUR EXPERIENCES

Our personal experiences add depth to the roots of our perceptions. Traumatic events, successes, failures, and relationships all leave their mark on how we perceive the world. A single betrayal can lead to a lifelong distrust of others, while a moment of unexpected kindness can restore our faith in humanity.

Life feels much lighter without trust issues and emotional baggage. You're not the official "scorekeeper" of life, even if you've felt or acted that way before. Forgiveness can be liberating. Choosing the high road—or aligning with a higher vibration—brings peace. Living in a state of love—for others and for yourself, flaws and all—is the highest vibration of all. Growth is what matters, and it's okay to be patient with yourself, to cheer yourself on, and to be your own best friend along the way.

The human brain has a tendency to create stories to make sense of events—even when those stories are incomplete or misleading. These stories shape our perceptions, which in turn shape our reality. By identifying these perceptions, we can begin to question and shift them, creating a more empowered and fulfilling life.

Below are hypothetical scenarios that illustrate how experiences can distort perception, and how recognizing this can help shift your mindset:

Amy was excluded from a group when she was young.

As a result, Amy may internalize the belief that she is unworthy of belonging, leading her to avoid social situations or sabotage relationships in adulthood—developing fear of intimacy, distrust, or difficulty with boundaries.

James experienced either physical or verbal harm or mistreatment during his childhood.

James may interpret anything that doesn't align with his desires as abuse, which could lead to hypersensitivity in relationships and difficulty distinguishing between actual harm and unmet expectations.

Alex experienced parental absence and neglect during childhood.

This early environment may lead Alex to believe that anyone who offers love will eventually leave—potentially causing behaviors that push others away and reinforcing a self-fulfilling prophecy of abandonment.

David grew up with financial hardship and scarcity.

David may believe that financial abundance is unattainable, leading to a scarcity mindset that prevents him from taking risks or seizing opportunities, thereby perpetuating financial struggles.

Jordan was diagnosed with a chronic illness in their early adulthood.

Jordan may believe that their illness defines their life, leading them to feel powerless and limited. This belief could result in avoiding new experiences or feeling unworthy of a fulfilling life despite their condition.

By recognizing and challenging these perceptions, you can shift your mindset and open the door to new possibilities. Understanding that these beliefs are not truths, but interpretations, allows you to rewrite the narrative and step into a more empowered version of yourself.

Revisiting and reframing these experiences allows us to release the weight of false narratives and create a new lens rooted in truth and possibility.

Has something happened in your life that made you believe you were less capable, lovable, or worthy than you truly are? _____

If so, write down the experience, the belief it created, and consider how that belief may not be serving you or your growth.

_____

_____

_____

_____

_____

If you were asked to look into the mirror right now and say, "I love you," would it feel uncomfortable or challenging? _____

If so, imagine looking into the mirror and seeing yourself at age five. Picture that small child clearly. What loving, kind, and comforting words would you say to them to make sure they knew how loved, valuable, and capable they truly are? Write this down as a message from your heart directly to theirs.

_____

_____

_____

_____

_____

THE ROLE OF BIOLOGY

Even our biology helps shape how we view the world. Research in genetics and neuroscience shows that certain traits and tendencies, such as a predisposition to anxiety or a natural inclination toward optimism, can be passed down through generations. While biology is not destiny, it's important to acknowledge how it interacts with our environment to shape our perceptions.

Understanding the biological factors that influence our lens can help us approach personal growth with compassion. For example, if you struggle with chronic anxiety, understanding it as a biological tendency rather than a personal failing can empower you to seek effective support and adopt strategies to manage it more proactively and with greater self-compassion.

Awareness is the key that unlocks the door to abundance. Acceptance is the realization that it's time to step through that doorway into a new space. Action is what propels you forward once inside—creating a conscious and deliberate shift in perception that can redirect the trajectory of your life.

Have you ever experienced anxiety, sensitivity, or grief? _____

If so, write down a tendency that isn't serving you, recognizing that it's not your fault, and consider how this awareness could help you shift toward a more positive perspective.

_____

_____

_____

_____

_____

_____

RECOGNIZING REACTIVE PATTERNS

Our past experiences often trigger emotional reactions that can hold us back from fully embracing life's opportunities. These reactions, rooted in unresolved experiences or emotional wounds, can cause us to respond to challenges in unhealthy or unproductive ways. For instance, you might find yourself repeatedly frustrated, defensive, or quick to retreat when facing difficulties—responses often linked to unresolved feelings from earlier experiences.

Have you ever experienced situations where you've felt frustrated, overwhelmed, or unable to move forward? _____

If so, write down three specific examples of these events, along with the emotional reactions they triggered.

_____

_____

_____

Write out any areas in your life where you currently feel stuck or frustrated.

_____

_____

In general, when facing a difficult challenge, what feelings or automatic responses typically arise? (For example: "I feel overwhelmed or defensive.")

_____

_____

Are you willing to continue the work of shifting your perceptions to overcome these obstacles and frustrations? _____

THE COST OF UNEXAMINED PERCEPTIONS

Operating with unexamined perceptions often means living on autopilot, leading to missed opportunities and unfulfilled potential. When we're unaware of the filters shaping our perceptions, we risk making decisions based on fear, bias, or outdated assumptions.

This can lead to staying in unfulfilling relationships, avoiding risks, or settling for far less than we're capable of—simply because we haven't paused to question the patterns driving our choices. If this sounds familiar, don't be hard on yourself. Most people have never been taught to examine their perceptions—let alone shown how to recognize their power. Developing this awareness is a *next-level skill*—one that requires both curiosity and courage.

The cost isn't just personal. On a societal level, unexamined lenses contribute to prejudice, inequality, and division. By becoming aware of and challenging our inherited perceptions, we not only transform our own lives but also help create to a more inclusive and understanding world.

Are you open to uncovering, discovering, and letting go of beliefs passed down to you that may no longer serve you? _____

If so, list one or two that you think could use some shifting.

_____

_____

_____

_____

_____

_____

REVISING OUR DISTORTED PERCEPTIONS

The good news is that we are not bound by the lens we inherit. While we can't change our past, we can choose how we interpret it and move forward. This process begins with self-awareness and a commitment to growth. Practical steps include:

Questioning Assumptions: Challenge the beliefs and narratives you've accepted as truth. Ask yourself, *"Is this belief serving me?"* and *"What evidence supports or contradicts it?"*

Seeking New Perspectives: Engage with people, ideas, and cultures different from your own. Exposure to diverse viewpoints can expand your understanding and reveal blind spots in your perception. It can also be fun approach life with an open mind and heart.

Practicing Gratitude: Often referred to as "thankfulness," gratitude might be the most powerful tool you can use. Focusing on what you appreciate in life shifts your attention from lack to abundance, helping you see possibilities rather than limitations. Cultivating an *Attitude of Gratitude* feels truly wonderful.

If you take a moment to reflect, there are countless things to be grateful for. Stumped? Start small—your fingers, toes, breath, or heartbeat. Then expand outward to include nature, food, kindness, or the simple gift of oxygen.

Gratitude is also contagious; surround yourself with grateful people, and you'll feel their positivity—and the same is true for you. The more grateful you are, the more you'll inspire and uplift those around you.

It's hard to have a bad day when anchored in gratitude. Try it for one day, or better yet, commit to 30 days, keeping in mind that gratitude is like fresh air—when you breathe it in and let it fill you up, you'll feel lighter, more grounded, and ready to embrace life's possibilities.

Rewriting Your Story: Replace limiting beliefs with empowering ones. For example, *"I'm not good enough"* can become *"I am capable and worthy of success."* Living as a "Debby Downer" means living in fear—a mindset that is not only disempowering but also harmful.

Fear-based thinking weakens the immune system and harms cardiovascular health. It also contributes to other physiological issues. It can even accelerate aging and lead to premature death. Choosing to rewrite your internal narrative helps you shift out of fear and into a mindset of empowerment, positivity, and vitality.

Are you willing to practice self-awareness, commit to growth, and choose to see things in a more empowering or positive way? _____

If so, write down a negative assumption you've had—and may still have—about yourself. For example, "I just can't achieve things like other people."

_____

_____

_____

_____

_____

_____

Now write down the opposite, for "I can achieve anything I work hard for."

_____

_____

_____

_____

_____

FINDING THE COURAGE TO CHANGE

The perceptions you've inherited are not your final destination. By exploring and reshaping them, you can break free from the limitations of your past and create a future aligned with your true potential. This transformative process requires courage, curiosity, and a willingness to question deeply held beliefs. Yet the rewards—a life filled with clarity, connection, and abundance—make the journey profoundly worthwhile.

As you continue your journey through this book, remember that every step you take toward understanding and transforming your lens brings you closer to the life you deserve. Your perceptions are the foundation of your reality, and you have the power to shape them in ways that inspire and uplift you.

Have you ever felt scared or uncomfortable when faced with making big changes in life? _____

If so, write about what fears or concerns arise when imagining a fundamental shift in your perspective, even if it means manifesting a life richer and more fulfilling than you've ever imagined.

_____
_____
_____
_____
_____
_____
_____
_____

EMBRACING THE SHIFT

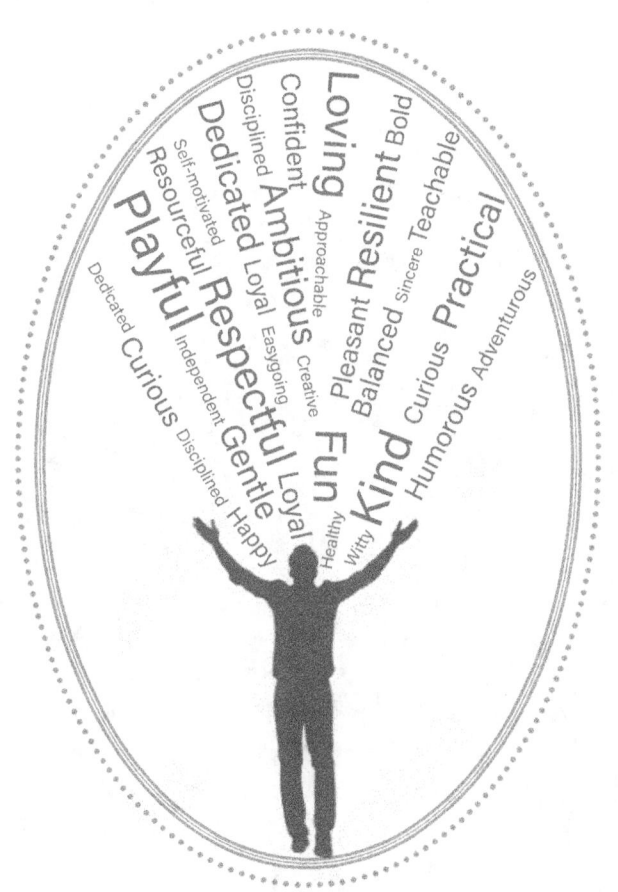

The Power of Mindset Shifting
EXPANDING YOUR AWARENESS

There once was a man who wandered through life carrying a dim lantern. It gave off just enough light to see a few steps ahead, but the world around him remained mostly in shadows. He grew used to the darkness—navigating cautiously, assuming danger lurked in every shadow.

One night, during a fierce storm, his lantern flickered out completely. Alone in unfamiliar woods, he panicked. He stumbled, tripped over roots, scraped his knees, and cursed the darkness.

Eventually, exhausted and unsure what to do, he stopped. He sat down, closed his eyes, and simply breathed. After a while, something told him to open them again.

To his astonishment, he could now see almost everything around him.

The trees, the path, even the curve of the mountain beyond—all faintly lit by the stars above. It had all been there the whole time.

By pausing and closing his eyes, he had allowed them to adjust. He hadn't changed the darkness—he had sharpened his perception. In stillness, he made space for a different kind of light to enter.

Life is full of pivotal moments—those brief, often unexpected instances when we pause, create space, and something clicks. Suddenly, we see things differently. These moments of clarity are the seeds of transformation. Recognizing when and how our existing perceptions may be holding us back is the first step toward changing them—and creating a life we love.

In this chapter, we'll explore how to identify limiting perceptions, understand the triggers that prompt *Perceptual Shifts*, and develop the self-awareness required to embrace new ways of seeing the world. By honing these skills, you can unlock greater joy, resilience, and abundance in your life.

Have you ever had a moment when something suddenly shifted, and you saw things in a different way? _____

If so, write down a pivotal moment—positive or negative—that influenced you. How did it shape your perspective, and what impact has it had on your life?

_____
_____
_____
_____
_____
_____
_____
_____
_____
_____
_____
_____
_____
_____
_____
_____

WHAT IS A PERCEPTUAL SHIFT?

A *Perceptual Shift* occurs when you change the way you interpret a situation, a relationship, or yourself. It's not about changing the facts but rather altering your perspective to see them in a new light.

For instance, a failed project might initially feel like a personal failure. But with a *Perceptual Shift*, you could view it as a valuable learning experience that prepares you for future success.

These shifts can be small—a realization during a conversation—or monumental, like a complete reevaluation of your life's purpose. What they all have in common is the power to open up new possibilities and pathways.

Have you ever looked back on a difficult experience, only to later see it in a more positive light? _____

If so, write down the experience and the perception you had immediately after it happened. Then, describe how your perspective has shifted and what that change has opened up for you.

_____
_____
_____
_____
_____
_____
_____
_____

SIGNS THAT IT'S TIME FOR A SHIFT

Sometimes, we're so entrenched in our perceptions that we don't realize a shift is necessary. However, there are often signs that our current way of seeing things isn't serving us. These signs may include:

Recurring Frustrations: If you find yourself stuck in the same conflicts or challenges over and over, it may be a sign that your perception of the situation could benefit from adjustment.

Emotional Turmoil: Persistent feelings of anger, sadness, or anxiety often stem from unexamined perceptions. Identifying the root cause can pave the way for a shift and open the door to greater peace, clarity, and emotional freedom.

Feeling Stuck: If life feels stagnant or unfulfilling, it's worth examining whether your perceptions are limiting your choices or holding you back from embracing new opportunities.

External Feedback: Sometimes, others' observations can point to blind spots in our perception. One indication that a shift may be necessary is when we find ourselves becoming defensive in response to the judgment of others. While it can be uncomfortable, constructive feedback can be a powerful catalyst for change.

Do you usually see things mostly from your perspective? _____

If so, write down a time this caused frustration or conflict and how considering their point of view could have created more understanding.

_____
_____
_____
_____

TRIGGERS THAT CAN SHIFT PERCEPTIONS

Triggers are events or experiences that challenge our existing perceptions and prompt us to see things differently. These can be positive, like an inspiring conversation, or negative, such as a personal setback. What matters is how we respond to these triggers.

Positive Triggers: These often come in the form of new opportunities, uplifting relationships, or moments of inspiration. For example, hearing a motivational speaker may ignite a shift in how you view your potential.

Negative Triggers: While painful, these can be equally transformative. A job loss, for instance, might lead you to reevaluate your career path and discover a more fulfilling direction.

Recognizing triggers as opportunities rather than obstacles is key to embracing *Perceptual Shifts*.

Has anyone ever told you something that changed the way you perceived a person, place, or situation in your life? _____

If so, write down an example and how it shifted your perspective.

_____
_____
_____
_____
_____
_____
_____
_____

DEVELOPING SELF-AWARENESS

Self-awareness is the foundation of recognizing and embracing *Perceptual Shifts*, which leads to greater abundance. Without it, we may remain blind to the ways our perceptions limit us. Developing self-awareness involves:

Mindfulness Practices: Activities like meditation, journaling, or simply taking time to reflect help you tune into your thoughts and feelings.

Active Listening: Paying attention to how others perceive you or the situation can provide valuable insights.

Identifying Patterns: Notice recurring themes in your thoughts or experiences. These patterns often reveal underlying perceptions that may benefit from a shift.

Seeking Feedback: Trusted friends, mentors, or therapists can offer perspectives that challenge your current way of seeing things.

Pausing When Agitated: Taking a moment to pause and reflect when emotions run high can reveal underlying perceptions that don't serve you. This simple practice often prevents reactive decisions and opens the door for clearer thinking and better choices.

Do you practice any of the above methods for developing self-awareness?
_____

If so, write down an example of how you've used one and how it has helped you gain a clearer perspective.

_____
_____
_____
_____

HOW TO RECOGNIZE A SHIFT

Recognizing and appreciating that a *Perceptual Shift* is occurring—or would be beneficial—is a process that unfolds gradually. Here are four common stages often experienced on the path from *"dis-ease"* to awakening:

Discomfort or Dissatisfaction: This is often the starting point. A sense that something isn't right can signal an opportunity to embrace a new perspective.

Awareness of Alternatives: Exposure to different ideas, people, or experiences can introduce you to new ways of seeing the world.

Reflection: Taking the time to process what you've learned or experienced is essential for internalizing new perspectives. Journaling helps solidify these insights, while practices like meditation can enhance the process by fostering clarity and allowing you to fully absorb the lessons.

Integration: Once you've embraced a new perception, it's important to apply it in your daily life, reinforcing the shift through action. Taking the time to recognize and appreciate each instance where you put this into practice strengthens the transformation and keeps you motivated.

Each stage of this journey builds upon the last, gradually guiding you from discomfort to newfound clarity and alignment, ultimately transforming the way you perceive and engage with the world.

Is there an area in your life where you're feeling discomfort or dissatisfaction at the moment? _____

If so, write down what that area is and how shifting your view could help bring clarity and relief.

_____
_____
_____

OVERCOMING RESISTANCE TO SHIFTING

Shifting perceptions can be challenging, as it requires confronting ingrained habits and beliefs. Resistance to change often arises from:

Fear of Letting Go: Surrendering familiar perceptions, even when limiting, can feel unsettling. However, walking through that discomfort—and choosing love over fear—opens the door to possibility and peace.

Ego Attachment: We often tie our identity to beliefs, making it difficult to admit when they're flawed. Embracing humility and releasing the need to be right strengthens self-awareness and fosters authenticity.

Social Pressure: Friends, family, or cultural norms may discourage new perspectives. Staying true to your growth is an act of courage that can inspire others to embrace their own journeys.

Habit: Old ways of thinking are comfortable. Shifting perceptions requires conscious effort and practice, but the payoff is well worth it.

Overcoming resistance starts with cultivating curiosity, focusing on the benefits of change, and seeking support from those who encourage growth. With consistent practice, supportive relationships, and faith in yourself, transformation is possible.

Have you ever had an interaction where your need to be right made the other person feel wrong? _____

If so, write down the situation and how allowing them to express their perspective without making them wrong could have changed the outcome.

_____

_____

_____

THE BENEFITS OF EMBRACING PERCEPTUAL SHIFTS

When we recognize and embrace shifts in perception, the benefits ripple through every aspect of our lives:

Greater Resilience: Seeing challenges as opportunities builds mental and emotional strength.

Enhanced Relationships: Shifting how you perceive others can deepen empathy, improve communication and help you disengage from toxic people or situations before you react impulsively.

Increased Creativity: A fresh perspective often sparks innovative ideas and solutions, opening the door to greater abundance.

Personal Growth: Becoming more comfortable with change fosters self-confidence and a sense of empowerment, boosting self-esteem.

Embracing *Perceptual Shifts* strengthens resilience, enriches relationships, sparks creativity, and invites abundance, leading to a more empowered and fulfilling life.

Can you see how simply learning to master Perceptual Shifting can benefit you in so many ways? _____

If so, of the benefits listed above, which one feels the most important to you, and why?

_____

_____

_____

_____

_____

EXAMPLES OF PERCEPTUAL SHIFTS IN ACTION

To illustrate the power of recognizing and embracing shifts, consider these real-life examples:

From Scarcity to Abundance: Oprah Winfrey grew up in poverty, Oprah Winfrey grew up in poverty, but by shifting her perception of what she could accomplish, she created opportunities that led to abundance. She's quoted as saying *"The greatest discovery of all time is that a person can change their future merely by changing their attitude."*

From Fear to Confidence: Winston Churchill, the iconic leader, had an intense fear of public speaking. By embracing the belief that through practice he could conquer his fear, he rose to become one of England's greatest orators. He famously stated, *"Of all the talents bestowed upon men, none is so precious as the gift of oratory."*

From Illness to Inspiration: Helen Keller lost her sight and hearing due to illness at just year old and later became a renowned author, speaker, and advocate for people with disabilities. She famously said, *"When one door of happiness closes, another opens; but often we look so long at the closed door that we do not see the one which has been opened for us."*

These real-life examples demonstrate how shifting perception can transform challenges into opportunities for growth, resilience and success.

Write down the number of the story that resonates with you most (1st, 2nd, etc.) _____

If you could choose to change any one thing in your life through **Perceptual Shifting***, what would it be and why?*

_____

_____

_____

OPENING YOUR MIND TO A NEW POINT OF VIEW

Recognizing the desire for a *Perceptual Shift* requires courage, but the rewards are immeasurable. By cultivating self-awareness, embracing triggers, and overcoming resistance, you can transform the way you see yourself, others, and the world.

Shifting perception isn't about ignoring reality but about choosing a perspective that empowers rather than limits you. Each moment offers the opportunity to reframe everything inside and around you—to see setbacks as step-ups, and to turn life's challenges into its greatest gifts. By consciously directing your focus, you reclaim your ability to shape your experiences and create a more rewarding and vibrant adventure.

As you continue this journey, remember: *each shift brings you closer to a life of greater joy, connection, and abundance.* The ability to see differently is a powerful tool for building the future you desire, and it all begins with recognizing the possibility for change.

Do you see that the potential to reframe events in your life in a positive way can actually create more abundance? _____

If so, write down one area of your life where shifting your perspective could open up many doors.

_____

_____

_____

_____

_____

_____

The Art of Reframing

FROM CHALLENGES TO OPPORTUNITIES

Two neighbors lived side by side in identical homes, each with the same view of a park filled with children, trees, and a winding path. Every morning, they opened their curtains to greet the day.

One neighbor would sigh and say, "Another noisy morning. Those kids are always yelling. The trees block the sunlight, and the path is always muddy." She started her days feeling agitated and drained.

The other neighbor would smile and say, "What a gift—a park filled with laughter and life. Those trees dance in the wind and shade the heat. The path shows the beauty of change." She began her days with gratitude and energy.

One day, a visitor asked, "How can two people look out at the same world and see it so differently?"

The smiling neighbor replied, "We don't look through the same window. Mine is cleaned daily with Perception Polish. You can make your own solution with a few simple ingredients: gratitude, curiosity, compassion, and a willingness to see things differently."

Reframing is a simple, yet profoundly transformative tool that helps us view our challenges, relationships, and even ourselves through a new lens. It's the ability to look at a situation and ask, *What if I saw this differently?"* The art of reframing helps us turn obstacles into opportunities, fears into strengths, and setbacks into lessons.

Unlike *Perceptual Shifting*, which seeks to rewire overarching beliefs and habitual thought patterns, reframing is a tool used to address individual moments and experiences, creating small but impactful changes in how you respond to life's ups and downs. Both approaches are powerful in their own right and work together to foster growth and resilience.

In this chapter, we will explore the principles of reframing, why it is such a powerful tool, and how to apply it effectively to create meaningful change in your life. By mastering the art of reframing, you can unlock new possibilities and experience greater resilience and fulfillment.

Have you ever turned a setback into a lesson by looking at it from a different perspective? _____

If so, write down a challenge you've experienced and how reframing it into a lesson has helped you grow or move forward.

_____
_____
_____
_____
_____
_____
_____
_____
_____
_____
_____
_____
_____
_____

CHANGING YOUR MINDSET

Reframing involves changing the meaning you assign to a situation. The facts remain unchanged, but the way you process and respond to them shifts. This practice can transform how you interpret challenges—for example, viewing failure not as evidence of incompetence but as a valuable opportunity for learning and growth.

For example, in relationships, reframing can help you move beyond blame or resentment. Instead of labeling your partner's actions as 'bad,' you might choose to find the silver lining—seeing them as opportunities for deeper understanding or connection. This subtle shift in how you view the situation fosters empathy and strengthens your bond.

The true power of reframing lies in its ability to transform not only how we feel but also how we act. By rewriting the story we tell ourselves about a challenge, we often discover new solutions and unlock peace of mind, freeing ourselves from the limits of a fixed mindset.

Have you ever initially seen something someone else did as "bad" but later realized it was actually beneficial in some way? _____

If so, write down the situation and how reframing it helped you see the positive side or benefit.

_____

_____

_____

_____

_____

_____

THE PERCEPTUAL SHIFT

WHY REFRAMING WORKS SO WELL

Reframing is effective because it taps into the brain's neuroplasticity—its ability to adapt and reorganize. When we consciously choose to view a situation differently, we create new neural pathways, which over time can shift our default ways of thinking.

Moreover, reframing disrupts negative thought patterns and replaces them with empowering narratives. This not only improves our mental and emotional well-being but also enhances our problem-solving abilities and creativity.

As we begin practicing the art of reframing and experiencing its rewards, the process becomes second nature. So we do it again and again—and feel better each time. Eventually, reframing becomes our automatic response whenever we feel any discomfort in our lives.

Additionally, reframing often leads to a positive shift in how we communicate with others, significantly enhancing our relationships. It serves as a powerful example of healthy communication, inspiring others to adopt similar practices.

Do you currently have a negative thought about someone that you can't shake because you believe it's true? _____

If so, write down who it is, what the thought is, and what might happen in your relationship with them if that thought simply disappeared.

_____

_____

_____

_____

THE PRINCIPLES OF REFRAMING

Recognize that your initial interpretation of a situation is not the only one. There are countless ways to view any experience. If you're uncomfortable with the way you're perceiving an event, someone's words or actions, or a feeling, take a moment to pause and explore alternative interpretations. Shifting how you frame the situation can lead to deeper understanding, emotional balance, and more constructive responses.

Focus on What You Can Control: Reframing often involves shifting your focus from what is beyond your control to what you can influence. Blaming is a red flag—it often signals an 'out-of-my-control' mindset—an opportunity to practice reframing.

By focusing exclusively on what's within your control—rather than trying to control people, places, or things—you can redirect your energy toward more empowering actions like letting go, setting boundaries, detaching with love, and responding thoughtfully rather than reacting impulsively.

Think of your personal power as existing within a *hula hoop* around you. Everything inside the hoop—your thoughts, actions, reactions, and perceptions—is within your control. However, the moment you step beyond that space, trying to control external circumstances or others, you're playing with fire.

The need to exert control where you have none often triggers resistance, conflict, or frustration. You may notice an external reaction from others, but the most significant reaction will always be within yourself—stress, anxiety, or resentment—because trying to control the uncontrollable is a losing battle. When you *stay inside your hula hoop*, you reclaim your energy, peace, and power, allowing others the space to do the same.

The same concept applies to living in the past or future. When your focus begins to dwell on regrets or anxieties about the future, you overlook the only place where life is truly happening: the present moment. It's no coincidence that the present is also called "the gift." Staying in your hula hoop also means embracing what's here and now, where your choices, growth, and joy actually exist.

Challenge Assumptions: Question the beliefs and assumptions that underlie your initial perspective. Are they accurate? Are they serving you? Do they make you feel frounded and empowered? If not, switch it up.

Embrace Curiosity: Approach reframing with an open and curious mindset. Ask yourself, *"What else could this mean?" "Is there another way I could look at this that doesn't leave me or anyone else feeling bad?"*

Practice Gratitude: Reframing is easier when you focus on the positive aspects of a situation, no matter how small. Writing down a few things each day in a **Gratitude Journal** is a great way to get used to focusing on the good, making it easier to reframe situations when it would be helpful.

If you feel stuck on how to start journaling or creating gratitude lists, I've developed *The Perceptual Shift Journal*, a companion to this book, designed to provide guidance and inspiration for these practices.

Is there a person, place, or thing that you can't control, and it's making you feel frustrated or hopeless? _____

Write out the situation, and think about how shifting your focus by taking the suggested actions in this book might make the situation better.

_____

_____

_____

_____

_____

REFRAMING CHALLENGES AS OPPORTUNITIES

Every challenge contains the seed of growth and transformation. By reframing difficulties as opportunities, you can shift from *"a victim mindset"* to one of empowerment. Consider taking these practical steps to guide your transformation:

Pause and Reflect: When faced with a challenge, take a deep breath. Extend it into a long, mindful pause. Now, step back and evaluate the situation. Don't speak, don't act, don't text, don't email. Wait until the emotional storm has passed and your discomfort has cleared before responding thoughtfully.

Identify the Lesson: Ask yourself, *"What can I learn from this?"* and *"How might this experience make me stronger?"* Grab a pen and your journal, then write down the situation and answer those questions. In every experience—especially when things don't go your way—look for the good and find gratitude.

For instance, when you stub your toe—yes, it hurts—but see it as an opportunity for a perceptual shift. Intentionally move into the ***Attitude of Gratitude*** by saying out loud, *"Thank you for my toe. Thank you for my bed."* Before long, you may even notice the pain starting to subside—and you can be grateful for that too.

By practicing this tool in situations big and small, you'll quickly find yourself becoming a ***Master Perceptual Shifter***.

Focus on Solutions: Shift your attention from the problem to potential solutions. Reframing often involves looking for the silver lining or a path forward. If you can't find a solution, try calling a friend who has a positive outlook on life and may be able to offer helpful suggestions.

Remember: ***what we focus on grows***—dwelling on the problem only magnifies it, while focusing on solutions leads us back to a place of empowerment and well-being.

As a word of caution, steer clear of negative individuals who reinforce a victim mindset without offering constructive insight. They only drive us away from peace, keeping us locked into the problem.

Celebrate Progress: Recognize and celebrate small victories along the way. This reinforces a positive outlook and motivates further growth. Share your progress with others on the same transformative journey—shifting perceptions to create abundance, freedom, and happiness.

By consistently reframing challenges as opportunities, you cultivate resilience, empowerment, and a mindset that seeks growth rather than defeat. Each moment of pause, reflection, and gratitude strengthens your ability to navigate life with confidence, ensuring that every experience—big or small—becomes a stepping stone toward greater wisdom, peace, and fulfillment.

Have you ever felt like a victim of someone else's behavior or life's circumstances? _____

If so, write down the situation and then reflect on how it would feel if you were never a victim again, but empowered, letting go of past hurt and negativity.

_____

_____

_____

_____

_____

_____

_____

_____

_____

THE ROLE OF LANGUAGE IN REFRAMING

The words we use to describe our experiences play a powerful role in shaping our perceptions. Empowering, positive language can help us reframe even the most difficult situations. For example, instead of saying, *"I failed,"* try, *"I learned something valuable."* Shift *"This is too hard"* to *"This is a chance to grow."* And instead of *"I'm stuck"* say, *"I'm figuring things out."*

Whether spoken aloud or repeated silently in your mind, negative language has a powerful way of dragging you down and keeping you trapped. It reinforces limiting beliefs and hinders your ability to evolve into the best version of yourself.

The words you choose shape your reality. By consciously rephrasing and reframing your thoughts, you'll experience a shift in energy—feeling lighter, more optimistic, and more aligned with your true potential. This practice not only strengthens your relationship with yourself but also deepens your love for both yourself and your life.

Have you ever said mean, negative, or unloving things to or about yourself? _____

If so, write down one way you negatively frame yourself, your actions, or your abilities, and then write down the opposite. For example, instead of "I'll never get ahead financially," say "I'm great at making money," or instead of "I'm just not good at relationships," say "I'm on my way to the healthiest, most loving relationship of my life."

_____

_____

_____

_____

REFRAMING IN RELATIONSHIPS

Reframing is especially powerful in relationships, where misunderstandings and conflicts often arise. By shifting your perspective, you can improve communication, deepen connection, and resolve tensions more effectively. Here are some tips:

Seek Understanding: Instead of assuming the worst, make an effort to understand the other person's perspective. Ask thoughtful questions, listen with compassion, and empathize—especially if you've faced similar situations before. If you feel tempted to judge, blame, or criticize, pause and try to put yourself in their shoes instead.

Assume Positive Intent: Reframe conflicts by assuming that the other person's actions are not meant to hurt you but are driven by their own challenges, desires or limitations.

Look for the Gift: Even in challenging relationships, there are often valuable lessons or opportunities for personal growth. Focus on cultivating equanimity and view every relationship as a chance to learn something new. That said, don't hesitate to temporarily detach when interactions become heated or unloving—prioritizing your well-being and allowing space for healthier communication later.

Have you ever had a relationship in the past that you think of as "bad"?
_____

If so, write down who that relationship was with and what you may have learned or gained from it, even if it was difficult.

_____
_____
_____
_____

THE RELUCTANCE TO REFRAME

While reframing is a powerful tool, it can be challenging to adopt at first. The "victim mentality," or tendency to blame, is deeply ingrained in our society, often reinforced by those around us. It's understandable, then, that for many of us, our initial response to conflict is to focus on others and what we perceive they've done wrong.

For some, victimhood can almost become an addiction—an unconscious habit of constantly identifying with struggle, injustice, and wrongdoing. We all know people who seem stuck in a loop of complaining about what's wrong and who has wronged them, rarely seeking solutions or taking accountability. This mindset can be incredibly limiting, keeping them in a perpetual state of frustration and powerlessness.

Gossip often extends this pattern, creating temporary connection through shared negativity rather than inspiring meaningful change. By becoming aware of when we slip into these behaviors, we can redirect our focus toward empowerment, healing, and meaningful change.

Breaking the cycle of blame requires recognizing these patterns and addressing the barriers that hinder personal growth. Common obstacles that get in the way of our ability to reframe include:

Attachment to the Story: We often cling to our initial interpretation of events, even when it's painful—because it feels familiar. Ask yourself, "Is this the only way to view the situation?" or "What if there's another explanation that feels less hurtful or more empowering?" By rewriting the story, you open yourself to new possibilities for understanding, healing, and growth.

Fear of Letting Go: Changing your perspective may require letting go of old beliefs or identities, which can feel unsettling. Be gentle with yourself—this process takes time, and it's okay to move at your own pace. Remember, growth doesn't have to be rushed; even small steps forward are meaningful.

THE PERCEPTUAL SHIFT

Cynicism: A negative mindset can make it difficult to see the value in reframing. Replace your cynical thoughts with empowering ones in order to change the internal script and cultivate gratitude.

Our Ego: Many of us cling to being *right* or *winning* because, in the past, being *wrong* or *losing* often brought pain. Ask yourself: Is being *right* or *winning* truly worth it if it leads to unhappiness for you or others? If your answer is no, you've already started the process of shifting your perception.

To overcome resistance, start small. Practice reframing minor annoyances or setbacks before tackling larger challenges. Over time, this practice will become a natural and empowering habit.

Have you ever found yourself blaming others or focusing on what's wrong instead of seeking solutions? _____

If so, write down someone you have recently blamed for something.

_____

What did you blame them for?

_____

_____

Were/are you mostly attached to your version of the story? _____

Were/are you worried that if you let go of this perspective, the issue could happen again? _____

Do you still feel upset or disappointed about what they did? _____

Do you think you are right and they are wrong? _____

If so, write down how putting yourself in their shoes might change your perception.

_____

_____

EXAMPLES OF REFRAMING IN ACTION

The Rejection Letter: Imagine applying for your dream job and receiving a rejection letter.

What's your first reaction?

_____

_____

How do you think you or most people would feel?

_____

_____

Instead of interpreting it as a personal failure, try reframing it as an opportunity to refine your skills or explore other exciting possibilities.

Seen in this new light, how would you feel receiving that same rejection letter?

_____

_____

This is a perfect illustration of reframing. It also opens the door to considering the role that *expectations* have on our perceptions.

One of the ways I get out of disappointment is to have a *Plan A, Plan B, and even a Plan C*, particulary when my hopes, desires or plans involve someone else. Here's an example of how it works:

If I've made plans to go out for dinner with a friend at my favorite Italian restaurant, instead of getting overly attached to that specific plan (Plan A), I also prepare a few alternatives so I can stay flexible and enjoy the night no matter what happens:

Plan A: Dinner at my favorite Italian restaurant.

Plan B: If my friend cancels or the restaurant is fully booked, I'll enjoy a cozy night in—maybe order takeout from a place I've been wanting to try and watch a movie I've been excited about.

Plan C: If my friend doesn't cancel but doesn't show up at all, I'll still treat myself to a great evening out—savoring the meal and indulging in dessert as a celebration of the fact that I had fun instead of getting angry or obsessing over being stood up.

By approaching the night this way, I stay relaxed, flexible, and open-minded. I reduce the chance of disappointment if things don't go exactly as planned— and I remind myself that joy can be found in any version of the experience when I let go of rigid expectations.

The Rainy Day: A sudden downpour might ruin your plans for a picnic, but reframing allows you to see it as a chance to enjoy a cozy day indoors or try something new. You can also look at how nurturing and wonderful rain is for our planet, getting you into the *Attitude of Gratitude*. Viewing the weather as an opportunity to tackle an inside task you've been postponing can reveal how the rain played a role in your achievement.

Of course, this kind of mental shift isn't always easy—especially when we're feeling disappointed or frustrated. But like any new skill, the more we practice reframing, the more natural and empowering it becomes. Eventually, it becomes second nature to look for the opportunity, rather than getting stuck in the setback.

The Difficult Relationship: A challenging relationship can feel draining, but reframing might help you see it as an opportunity to practice patience, empathy, or boundary-setting. Some of my most challenging relationships have offered the greatest opportunities for growth, helping me evolve into a better version of myself.

When my first wife and I separated and later divorced, my dreams of a lifelong family were shattered—but I knew in my heart that somehow things would work out. And they did. I ended up marrying my high school sweetheart and went from being the father of one child to the father of four—literally four times the love, laughter, and joy I thought I'd lost.

Have you ever experienced a situation or interaction you initially perceived as "terrible," but later discovered a silver lining? _____

If so, write down a recent situation you're currently perceiving as "bad" and take a moment to imagine one positive outcome or lesson that it may hold.

_____
_____
_____
_____
_____
_____
_____
_____
_____
_____
_____
_____
_____
_____
_____
_____

PRACTICAL EXERCISES FOR REFRAMING

The Gratitude Journal: Each morning or evening, write down at least three things you're grateful for and one challenge you recently reframed as an opportunity. If you're struggling with ideas or unsure how to get started, you'll find helpful examples and guidance in *The Perceptual Shift Journal*—a companion to this book for those seeking more direction.

The *"What Else Could It Mean?"* Exercise: When faced with a difficult situation, list three alternative interpretations or perspectives. Here's an example: If your boss gives you critical feedback on your work, instead of viewing it negatively, try reframing it in one of the following ways:

- *They see potential in you and want to help you grow, or*
- *They might be under stress and unintentionally projecting it onto the situation, or*
- *They simply have different expectations or a perspective you hadn't considered.*

By choosing to see the feedback differently, you can focus on the opportunity to grow and improve, rather than spiraling into thoughts like:

- *"I'm bad," or*
- *"I can't do anything right," or*
- *"I should have never taken this stupid job."*

Role Reversal: When you're feeling uncomfortable about something in your life, take a moment to reflect and write down the entire experience and the range of emotions you're going through.

Now, imagine you are giving advice to a friend in your situation. What perspective or solution would you suggest? Try writing down the situation in your journal, then reflect on whether the advice you'd give is something you can apply to your own life.

Appreciation: Make it a daily habit to show your appreciation for something someone else has done each day. It can be a compliment in person, a text message or act of kindness. Appreciating others strengthens connections, enhance morale, and encourages positive behaviors, fostering goodwill and mutual respect in all your relationships.

These reframing exercises provide simple tools to shift your perspective and create positive outcomes. By practicing gratitude, exploring alternative viewpoints, and showing appreciation for others, you can break free from limiting beliefs and embrace a mindset of growth.

Do you often experience some kind of challenge or uncomfortable situation in your daily life? _____

If yes, how do you feel that the exercises above could help you transform your daily challenges into opportunities?

_____

_____

_____

_____

_____

_____

_____

_____

_____

_____

REFRAMING AS A LIFELONG PRACTICE

The art of reframing is not a one-time skill but an ongoing practice. As you integrate it into your daily life, you will find that challenges become less daunting, relationships become more fulfilling, and your sense of purpose deepens. And perhaps, most importantly, you'll begin to like yourself more.

Reframing is like training a muscle—it grows stronger with repetition, awareness, and patience. Some days, it will come easily, while on others, old habits of thinking may resurface. That's part of the process. The key is to recognize when you've fallen into limiting thought patterns and gently guide yourself back to a more empowering perspective through the act of reframing. Over time, this practice becomes second nature, helping you navigate life with greater ease and emotional resilience.

By learning to see the world differently, you open yourself to endless possibilities for growth, joy, and abundance. Reframing empowers you to be the author of your own story, creating a life that reflects your highest potential.

Do you think reframing difficult experiences can help you manifest a happier, more fulfilled, and abundant life? _____

If so, write down what you can start doing today to reframe your experiences, such as pausing when you feel upset, listening from the other person's perspective, or focusing on gratitude in challenging situations.

_____

_____

_____

_____

_____

Transforming Through Transitions
EMBRACING THE CHANGE

A young caterpillar lived on a lush green leaf, content with his routine—eating, crawling, resting in the sun. He'd never ventured far, never needed to. The leaf provided everything he needed.

One day, dark clouds gathered. A fierce wind blew in, shaking the tree violently. The caterpillar clung tightly, terrified. The storm tore through the branches, and in one final gust, his beloved leaf was ripped away, carrying him through the air and far from home.

When the wind finally settled, he found himself on a strange, unfamiliar branch. Nothing looked the same. The leaves were tougher, the sun hit differently, and worst of all, he didn't recognize anything—he felt lost, broken, and certain the best part of life was behind him.

But with no choice, he adapted. He began to move, to explore. The new leaves nourished him in ways he never expected. Little did he know, the storm had not taken something from him—it had carried him into the heart of his becoming, toward a life more expansive and abundant than he ever thought possible.

In time, he felt the call to rest—and he did. When he emerged, he had wings. With them, his perspective shifted. He rose above the branches and saw, for the first time, the forest—lush, vast, and alive with beauty. What once felt like loss became a gateway to limitless abundance.

Life is full of change—some planned, some unexpected. While many of us fear change, it is an inevitable part of the human experience. In fact, growth and transformation depend on our ability to adapt to new circumstances. When we cease fighting change, it allows us to unlock hidden opportunities, build resilience, and discover parts of ourselves we never knew existed.

In this chapter, we will explore why change is so challenging, how to reframe it as a positive force, and practical strategies to embrace it. By the end, you will see change not as something to fear or resist but as an ally on your journey to abundance and fulfillment.

Do you feel that change can sometimes be scary or overwhelming? _____

If so, write down a recent "scary" change you walked through that turned out not to be nearly as bad as you thought it would be, or maybe it really ended up being good.

_____

_____

_____

_____

_____

_____

Reflect on what you learned from that experience.

_____

_____

_____

_____

_____

_____

_____

WHY CHANGE CAN BE SO FRIGHTENING

Our resistance to change is rooted in both biology and psychology. The human brain is wired to seek stability and predictability. When faced with uncertainty, the amygdala—the brain's fear center—activates, triggering a fight-or-flight response. As a result, change can feel threatening, even when it holds the potential for growth and new opportunities.

On a psychological level, change challenges our sense of identity and control. Letting go of the familiar often means stepping into the unknown, which can evoke feelings of vulnerability and create anxiety. Understanding these natural responses is the first step toward overcoming the fear of change.

This innate resistance to change is also reinforced by past experiences and societal conditioning. Many of us have been taught to equate stability with security, making any deviation from the known feel risky or even dangerous. Additionally, past failures or disappointments can create subconscious fears that change will lead to loss rather than growth. However, when we recognize that discomfort is a natural part of transformation—realizing it opens the door to abundance—we can begin to reframe change as an opportunity rather than a threat.

Did you learn anything new about the amygdala and its role in how we respond to change? _____

If so, write down a situation you've been worried about, where your amygdala (fear center) is triggered, and then consider what potential abundance could come instead of imagining the worst-case scenario.

_____

_____

_____

_____

THE BENEFITS OF OPENING UP TO CHANGE

While change can be uncomfortable, it is also a powerful catalyst for growth. When we embrace change, we:

Develop Resilience: Each time we navigate and embrace change, we strengthen our ability to adapt and overcome challenges, building confidence in our capacity to handle whatever comes our way.

Discover New Opportunities: Change often brings unexpected possibilities that can lead to personal and professional growth. Every obstacle is an opportunity in disguise—it's up to us to find it.

Deepen Self-Awareness: Change invites us to reflect. Writing down your thoughts can bring clarity and help shift your perspective.

Foster Creativity: New circumstances challenge us to think differently, sparking innovation and problem-solving. Often, the best experiences in life come from changes we initially resisted.

Build Meaningful Connections: Change often brings new people into our lives, enriching our relationships and broadening our perspectives.

Have you ever met a new person that enriched your life as a result of a change that you initially resisted? _____

If so, write down what the change was, who the person was, and how they made your life better.

_____

_____

_____

_____

_____

REFRAMING CHANGE AS A POSITIVE FORCE

Perspective reframing is a powerful tool for shifting our perspective on change. Instead of viewing it as a disruption, we can see it as an opportunity for growth and discovery. Here are some ways to reframe change:

Focus on the Benefits: Ask yourself, *"What opportunities might this change bring?"* or *"How could this help me grow?"* Stay open to the possibility that this change could lead to something good.

Embrace Curiosity: Approach change with a sense of wonder, asking, *"What can I learn from this experience?"* Change is often an opportunity to become a better version of yourself.

Trust the Process: Change is constant—and often leads to something better. The more you trust it, the more at ease you'll feel.

Celebrate Flexibility: Recognize that your ability to adapt is a strength that will serve you in every aspect of life. Navigating change with dignity and grace will make you stronger.

The takeaway here is that, by reframing any fear of the future, change becomes empowering. You have the ability to master change in a way that creates the best possible outcome in every situation you face.

Do you get upset when things don't go as planned? _____

If so, in what ways could your life improve if change no longer upset you?

_____
_____
_____
_____

COMMON TYPES OF CHANGE & HOW TO NAVIGATE THEM

Change shows up in many forms, from career transitions to personal loss. Each type of change presents unique challenges and opportunities. Here are some common scenarios and strategies for navigating them:

CAREER CHANGES

Challenge: Leaving a familiar role or starting a new one can be daunting.

Strategy: Focus on the skills and experiences you bring to the table. Use this transition as an opportunity to align your work with your values and passions, and remember that every new beginning holds the potential for something greater to unfold.

RELATIONSHIP CHANGES

Challenge: Breakups, new relationships, or shifts in family dynamics can evoke strong emotions.

Strategy: Avoid passive-aggressive behavior. Instead, practice open communication, set healthy boundaries, and give yourself time to process and heal. Being kind and loving to others is important, but not at the expense of being kind and loving to yourself first.

RELOCATION

Challenge: Moving to a new place can disrupt routines and social connections, often creating fear and uncertainty about fitting in or finding a sense of belonging.

Strategy: Explore your new environment with curiosity, and actively seek opportunities to build community. Remind yourself that this change holds the potential for exciting new experiences, personal growth, and meaningful connections.

PERSONAL GROWTH

Challenge: Letting go of old habits or beliefs can feel uncomfortable.

Strategy: Celebrate small victories and remind yourself that growth is a lifelong journey. Shedding thoughts, attitudes, feelings and actions that no longer serve you can be both uplifting and invigorating.

UNEXPECTED LOSS

Challenge: Coping with the loss of a loved one, job, or dream is deeply painful and can feel overwhelming, shaking your sense of stability.

Strategy: Seek support from loved ones or a qualified therapist, allowing yourself to grieve while also finding ways to honor your experience and move forward. Grief is natural, but staying in it too long can overshadow what matters most. Take small steps forward, even if it feels difficult at first—sometimes, *faking it until you make it* can reestablish momentum. The goal issn't to erase the pain, but to move through it, appreciate the journey, and recognize it as a powerful catalyst for growth.

Change tests our resilience, shifts our perspectives, and challenges us to grow. Every transition—career shifts, relationship changes, relocation, or loss—brings both hardship and possibility. Navigating change is ultimately about mindset: embracing it with courage, focusing on what we can control, and trusting in its transformative power.

Instead of resisting change, lean into it as an invitation for growth. Step forward with confidence, knowing that change isn't here to break you—it's here to shape, strengthen, and transform you.

Do you think that if you started embracing change more often, instead of resisting it, things would feel more comfortable in your life? _____

If so, write down a recent change you resisted and the difficulties you experienced as a result of this resistance.

_____

_____

_____

BUILDING RESILIENCE THROUGH CHANGE

Resilience is the ability to adapt and thrive in the face of adversity. It's a skill that can be strengthened through intentional practices. Here are some ways to build resilience:

Cultivate a Growth Mindset: Believe in your capacity to learn and adapt. View challenges not as roadblocks but as opportunities for personal growth. Incorporating positive affirmations can reinforce this mindset and help rewire your internal dialogue toward possibility and progress.

Each morning, after a few mindfulness rituals, I raise my hands to the sky, open them like a chalice, and say: *"I open myself up to abundance! Abundance of finance, romance, love, compassion, goodness, laughter, creativity, and everything the universe wants for me. I'm getting out of the way so you can pour it all in. I love my life!"*

This simple affirmation, practiced consistently over the years, has had a profound effect on my life. It serves as a daily reminder to embrace possibilities, invite positivity, and trust the process of growth and abundance. Try creating a similar ritual that resonates with you and see how it can transform your outlook and experiences.

Practice Self-Compassion: Be kind to yourself during times of change. Acknowledge your feelings and remind yourself that it's okay to struggle. Treat yourself to something nice occasionally.

Stay Connected: Lean on a positive, loving support network for encouragement and perspective. Sharing your experiences with like-minded individuals can make change feel less overwhelming, especially when surrounded by those who prioritize personal growth, gratitude, and an abundance mindset.

Get involved with groups that focus on shifting perspective, abundance, compassion, and peace. For example, join yoga classes, meditation groups, or even create a group of friends to journey through this book together.

Commit to connecting with them regularly, as consistency is key. Yes, it takes effort to find, join, and maintain these connections, but the reward—a paradigm shift that can redirect your entire life toward a more joyful, abundant, and fulfilling path—is immeasurable.

Focus on Your Strengths: Reflect on past changes you've successfully navigated and use those experiences as evidence of your resilience. Celebrate your victories—big or small—and share them with others who uplift and encourage you along your journey of personal growth. Doing so reinforces your commitment to this path and highlights how *Perceptual Shifting* is positively impacting your life. Not only does this strengthen your resolve, but it also serves as a powerful inspiration for others to embrace their own transformative journeys.

Maintain Healthy Habits: Incorporating practices that support your overall well-being can make a world of difference when facing life's changes and challenges. Regular exercise, quality sleep, balanced nutrition, wellness routines, meditation, affirmations, laughter, hobbies, and meaningful work are all essential elements that significantly enhance the quality of your relationships, outlook on life, and overall well-being.

Building resilience through change means embracing a growth mindset, practicing self-compassion, and staying connected with a supportive network. By focusing on strengths and maintaining healthy habits, you can navigate challenges and change with greater ease and confidence.

Do you believe that becoming stronger and more adaptable through change can help you thrive rather than just survive? _____

If so, write down one practice or habit from the reading that resonates with you and how you can incorporate it into your daily life to strengthen your ability to handle change.

_____

_____

PRACTICAL STRATEGIES FOR ACCEPTING CHANGE

Going with the flow when changes occur requires both mindset shifts and actionable steps. Here are some strategies to help you navigate transitions with confidence:

Break It Down: Large changes can feel overwhelming. Break them into smaller, manageable steps to make the process feel more achievable. Write them down so they aren't just swirling around in your mind.

Stay Present: Mindfulness involves being fully present in the moment, focusing on what you're doing, feeling, and experiencing without judgment. It's about savoring life's small, meaningful moments instead of rushing to the next task.

For instance, in *The Miracle of Mindfulness* by Thich Nhat Hanh, he describes the act of washing dishes as a mindfulness practice. Instead of rushing to finish so you can eat or move on to something else, focus on the process: feel the warmth of the water, notice the smoothness of the soap, and appreciate the clean, shiny surface of each dish. By directing your attention to the present moment, even mundane tasks can become opportunities for gratitude and peace.

Incorporating practices like this into your daily routine can help you find joy and meaning in the simplest of activities, fostering a sense of calm and presence that extends into every aspect of your life.

Set Intentions: Clarify and write down your goals and values to guide your decisions, recognizing that there are many ways to set and work toward your goals.

Whether you prefer creating detailed plans, visualizing your future, or focusing on daily small steps, the key is to align your efforts with what truly matters to you. It's also perfectly okay if your goals or intentions evolve over time—growth is a natural part of the journey.

Later in this book, you'll explore a section called *"Creating a New Roadmap,"* which offers practical guidance to help you navigate this process.

Seek Support: Don't be afraid to ask for help. Friends, mentors, and professional coaches can offer invaluable guidance and encouragement on your journey. You don't need to act on every piece of advice, but consider what resonates with you and adapt it to suit your unique path, ensuring it aligns with your goals and values. In other words, take what you like and leave the rest.

Celebrate Progress: Acknowledge your efforts and achievements along the way. Celebrating small wins builds momentum and confidence. Writing down victories and sharing them is empowering. Yes, I've said this before—and I'll say it again—because repetition is what makes this journey successful.

Remember: ***doing your best is always enough***—regardless of what others may think. By focusing on small wins, you can find the kernel of good in every effort and overcome the *"dis-ease"* that perfectionism creates. Progress—not perfection—is the key to growth and fulfillment.

Accepting change requires both mindset shifts and practical steps. By breaking down large changes into manageable parts, staying present through mindfulness, setting clear intentions, seeking support, and celebrating small wins, you can navigate transitions with greater confidence. These strategies empower you to embrace change, stay focused on what truly matters, and discover growth and fulfillment along the way.

Do you have mentors or individuals in your life who are good at navigating change and seem to love their lives? _____

If so, list those individuals below. If not, are you willing to find new people who can support your efforts to navigate a more empowered life?

_____

_____

THE ROLE OF GRATITUDE DURING SEASONS OF CHANGE

Gratitude is a powerful tool for navigating change. By focusing on what you appreciate, you can shift your perspective from loss to abundance. Here are some ways to cultivate gratitude during times of change:

Keep a Gratitude Journal: Write down three things you are grateful for each day, even if they seem small—maintaining an *Attitude of Gratitude* is incredibly powerful. Being grateful is a cornerstone of *Perceptual Shifting*.

Express Appreciation: Show gratitude through a note, a thank-you, or a small gesture. A simple text like, "*Thinking of you and feeling grateful to have you in my life*," can be a powerful way to uplift others.

Find Silver Linings: Seek the positive in your situation, even if they aren't immediately clear—this is key to *Perceptual Shifting*. One effective way to do this is through random acts of kindness, which can shift your focus, lift your spirit, and reveal hidden good in difficult moments.

Reflect on Growth: Think about how past changes have shaped you and the lessons they've offered. Acknowledge your victories—moments you shifted from negativity to positivity. This builds clarity, resilience, and a mindset of abundance.

Gratitude helps shift your focus from loss to abundance during times of change. By keeping a gratitude journal, expressing appreciation, and seeking silver linings, you can foster a positive mindset, strengthen resilience, and embrace change with clarity and optimism.

Do you believe that practicing gratitude can help you navigate change with a more positive and empowered mindset? _____

If so, write down two things you're grateful for that happened today.

_____ _____

CHANGE AS A CATALYST FOR ABUNDANCE

Embracing change is not always easy, but it is essential for growth and transformation. By understanding the nature of change, reframing it as an opportunity, and cultivating resilience, you can navigate life's transitions with confidence and grace.

Change isn't an enemy to fear—it's a teacher to welcome. Resistance only creates struggle. It's like clinging onto the bumper of a moving car. If someone is driving away, you won't stop them—you'll only get dragged and hurt.

When you embrace change, you open the door to endless possibilities for joy, connection, and abundance. Remember, every ending is also a new beginning, and the best is yet to come.

Can you relate to the idea that when we struggle against what's happening in life, it's like being dragged behind a car? _____

If so, write about the last time you resisted change, and reflect on what would have been a better way to find acceptance and move forward with less pain and suffering.

_____

_____

_____

_____

_____

_____

_____

_____

INSPIRING STORIES OF EMBRACING CHANGE

The Relationship Reinvention: After the death of his first wife, Alice Hathaway Lee, in 1884, Theodore Roosevelt was devastated. He withdrew from public life for a time to grieve but later found love again with Edith Kermit Carow, a childhood friend whom he married in 1886. Together, they had five children and shared a strong, supportive marriage. Roosevelt's ability to embrace life and love once more after such profound loss is a testament to his resilience, showing that even after heartbreaking loss, it is possible to build a new and fulfilling chapter in life.

The Career Reinvention: Jon Hamm spent years working as a bartender while struggling to find acting roles. After being fired from his bartending job, he embraced the change and fully committed to his acting career. His big break came when he was cast as Don Draper in *Mad Men*, a role that catapulted him to fame and earned him numerous accolades. Hamm's resilience and willingness to adapt to the change turned what seemed like a setback into a life-changing opportunity—proving that sometimes getting pushed out of your comfort zone can lead to unexpected success.

The Health Transformation: Bethany Hamilton, a professional surfer who lost her arm in a shark attack, did not let the loss define her. Instead, she returned to the sport she loved, inspiring millions with her resilience and determination. She became a powerful advocate for others facing physical challenges, proving that even the most difficult circumstances can be turned into opportunities for growth, influence, and impact.

Have you ever struggled with a difficult change in the area of finance, romance, or health? _____

If so, write down one good thing that has come out of it.

_____

_____

_____

A WORD OF CAUTION ON TRYING TO CHANGE OTHERS

Being open to change fosters growth, adaptability, and new opportunities. While personal transformation can strengthen relationships, trying to control others often leads to tension and resentment.

It's natural to want to change people, places, and things—but life and others can function just fine without your interference. People resist being changed by others—just as you likely do—making this a common source of conflict. Instead, focusing on *self-change* fosters healthier, more fulfilling connections.

Some situations, however, do require leadership. Parents must set boundaries for their children's well-being, and managers must hold others accountable to maintain a productive workplace. Like staying in control while driving, knowing when to lead and when to let go is key.

Rather than focusing on what others should change, turn inward and tend to your own thoughts and actions. Staying in your own *"hula hoop"*—respecting personal boundaries—creates space for growth. By accepting change and shifting your focus inward, you open the door to personal transformation and stronger, more authentic relationships.

Do you now understand that the greatest opportunities for a happier, more abundant, and peaceful life come from working on changing our actions, reactions, and well-being, rather than trying to change the behavior of others? _____

If so, write about a situation where you tried to change someone else and how focusing on your own actions instead could have created a better outcome.

_____

_____

_____

Gratitude as a Compass
THE JOURNEY TOWARD ABUNDANCE

A weary traveler wandered through a dense and unfamiliar forest. She had no clear direction, no path forward, and a satchel full of heavy stones—**regret, resentment, fear, and self-pity**—each one picked up over years of trying to navigate life without ever quite finding peace.

One evening, she came upon a clearing where an old woman sat beside a fire. Without speaking, the woman pulled something from her cloak—a **flat, clear baseplate**—and held it out.

The traveler took it, puzzled. *"What is this?"*

"It's the foundation of a compass," the woman replied. *"You'll need it. But first, a trade."*

"A trade?"

"A stone," the woman said gently. *"Something you've been carrying too long."*

The traveler hesitated. Her regrets had been with her for so long, they felt like part of her. But something in the woman's eyes made her pause. Slowly, she reached into her satchel and handed over the heavy stone marked *Regret*.

The woman accepted it and passed her the baseplate, along with a weathered map. *"Now go,"* she said. *"Follow the trail east until you reach the river. There you'll find a man who can help with the next piece."*

By the river, the traveler found a quiet old man tending a small fire. When she showed him the baseplate, he nodded knowingly and handed her a **compass dial**, the part that would one day hold a magnetic needle. *"It won't function yet,"* he said, *"but it's essential. I'll trade it to you for another stone."*

She reached into the satchel and, with some hesitation, pulled out **Resentment**. The moment she let it go, her chest felt a little more open. A little more free.

He didn't just give her the dial—he pointed to the horizon. "Follow the river," he said. "At the end of it, you'll see a grove. There's a large stone at its base—stop there. Someone will be waiting."

When she reached the grove, sunlight filtered through the trees, casting golden light on the grass. Sitting beneath the branches was a small child, quietly stacking stones.

The child smiled and held up a **magnetic needle**, shimmering slightly as if alive.

"This will help you find your way," the child said, "*but only if you're ready to give up your fear.*"

The traveler laughed softly. "*That one's been with me forever.*"

"*I know,*" said the child. "*But it's not helping you anymore.*"

She closed her eyes, held her stone of *Fear*, and with a deep breath—released it. The child placed the needle in her hand. As it clicked into the dial, the compass pulled gently, surely, toward something unseen—but certain.

Before she turned to leave, the child pointed beyond the grove. "Climb to the top of that hill," they said, "where the sun touches the stones. There you'll find the final piece—and someone who will help you see what you've been carrying all along."

The final leg of her journey led her up a hillside, where the golden light of late afternoon poured over the rocks like honey. At the top, seated on a smooth stone worn by time and wind, was a quiet monk with kind eyes and a weathered face that held both age and youth at once.

He wore simple robes the color of river clay and moss, and his long, silver

GRATITUDE AS A COMPASS

hair was tied loosely at the nape of his neck. Beside him, a wooden bowl of water caught sunlight from a nearby aquifer that trickled through stone.

He looked at her gently and said, "*You look tired. Lost for too long. It's been an arduous trip. Sit. Rest your head.*"

Wordlessly, he handed her a carved wooden cup, filled with the cool, mineral-rich water. She drank, and the exhaustion of the entire journey washed over her. She sat beside him on the warm rock and pulled out the now almost-complete compass.

The monk reached into a pouch at his side and handed her the final piece: a **rotating bezel ring**, simple yet precise. She fit it gently into place, and for a moment, the compass pulsed with energy—like it had taken a breath.

She watched as the needle came alive. It began to spin. First slowly, then faster. It spun in wide circles, endlessly, searching. Not pointing north. Not settling. Just spinning. It began to make her dizzy. She blinked, watching it whirl, and felt her whole body begin to soften. The journey, the hills, the stones—all of it drifted like mist. And then—She closed her eyes.

She awoke in her own bed, the morning sun soft against her face. Her satchel was gone. The forest, gone. No map, no monk, no compass. Just the steady rise and fall of her breath… and the unmistakable feeling that something inside her had shifted.

She sat up slowly, as if waking from a dream—but with the kind of clarity that dreams rarely leave behind. And though she knew it had all been a dream, she also recognized the symbolism. Each person along her path didn't give her direction—they helped her build the tool to find her own. It was time to start heading in a new direction—away from regret, resentment, fear, and self-pity… and toward something far more powerful. She felt it like a quiet hum in her chest: Gratitude.

Gratitude for the journey. Gratitude for the lesson. And gratitude for the extraordinary life still waiting to unfold. And though there there was no compass in her hand now, she realized she didn't need one. Because she knew exactly where she was going.

Gratitude is more than just a fleeting feeling; it is a profound way of seeing the world that can transform your life. By shifting your focus from what you lack to what you have, gratitude becomes a compass that guides you toward joy, abundance, and fulfillment. It is not about ignoring challenges but about choosing to see the blessings within them, and releasing those things you ultimately have no control over anyway.

Gratitude acts as a guiding force, much like signposts along a winding path, pointing us in the direction of greater peace, fulfillment, and abundance. When we intentionally cultivate gratitude, it shifts our perspective and gently steers us away from negativity, self-doubt, and fear. It helps us recognize that even in difficult moments, there is something valuable to take away. Living in the **Attitude of Gratitude** transforms how we see life—not as something happening *to* us, but as something unfolding *for* us.

In this chapter, you'll explore the science behind gratitude, how it shapes our perceptions, and practical ways to integrate it into daily life. By the end, you'll discover how gratitude can serve as a powerful tool for navigating life's challenges and manifesting your deepest desires.

Do you feel better when thinking of the blessings in your life, rather than focusing on the hardships? _____

If so, write down something great going on in your life right now and how it feels to write it out.

_____

_____

_____

_____

THE SCIENCE OF GRATITUDE

Gratitude has been extensively studied in the fields of psychology and neuroscience. Research shows that practicing gratitude activates the brain's reward system, releasing feel-good chemicals like dopamine and serotonin. This not only boosts mood but also strengthens our ability to bounce back after setbacks, fostering overall well-being.

A landmark study by Emmons and McCullough, titled *Counting Blessings Versus Burdens: An Experimental Investigation of Gratitude and Subjective Well-Being in Daily Life*, found that individuals who kept a weekly gratitude journal reported greater optimism, improved sleep, and increased overall happiness compared to those who focused on daily hassles.

Another study by Wong and Brown, *How Gratitude Changes You and Your Brain*, suggests that gratitude can serve as a protective factor against anxiety and depression, helping individuals maintain a more balanced emotional state.

These studies—and many others—affirm that gratitude is not just a fleeting emotion, but a powerful psychological tool with long-term benefits for both mind and body.

Not to mention, it's a lot more fun than being upset or uptight!

Have you ever suffered from anxiety, also known as a feeling of unease or worry? _____

If so, write down a recent situation where anxiety took hold and how much time you spent in that feeling. How could you have decreased this time?

_____

_____

_____

_____

HOW GRATITUDE SHAPES PERCEPTION

Our perceptions are profoundly shaped by where we direct our attention. Like a magnifying glass, what we focus on appears larger. When we fixate on life's problems, they can easily feel overwhelming. This applies not only to our own lives but also to the problems of others—and even the world at large.

However, when we focus on gratitude, we train our minds to notice and appreciate the positive aspects of life. This doesn't mean ignoring challenges, but rather balancing them with an awareness of the good that exists alongside them.

For example, during a difficult day at work, gratitude might help you recognize a supportive colleague who offered help, or the opportunity to learn something new. Over time, this practice shifts your default perspective, making you more optimistic and solution-focused.

Do you understand the concept of a magic magnifying glass that makes what you're looking at bigger? _____

If so, assign a ratio to what your magnifying glass is currently focused on—negative versus positive. For example, 30% negative / 70% positive. Then, reflect on the ratio you'd like to aim for moving forward.

_____

_____

_____

_____

_____

_____

GRATITUDE AS A DAILY PRACTICE

Making gratitude a habit requires intention and consistency. Like any meaningful practice, it takes effort to shift from occasional appreciation to a daily mindset of thankfulness. By consciously incorporating gratitude into your routine, you reinforce positive neural pathways, making it easier to recognize and appreciate life's blessings, both big and small. Here are some practical ways to cultivate gratitude in your daily life:

Morning Reflections: Start your day by focusing on gratitude. Reflect on what you're thankful for, no matter how small, to set a positive tone for the hours ahead. This simple practice can shift your mindset, creating a foundation of optimism and abundance for the day. Write down some gratitude in your journal.

Gratitude Immersion: Replace any looming negative thoughts and feelings with a sense of gratitude by soaking up positivity through daily doses of inspiring books, podcasts, motivational speakers, or TV shows. Immerse yourself in content that uplifts, empowers, and inspires. By consistently filling your mind with these positive influences, you can gradually shift your perspective and replace negativity with loving, empowering thoughts.

Express Gratitude to Others: Take the time to thank someone who has made a difference in your life. A heartfelt note or a simple "thank you" can strengthen your connection and uplift both of you.

Practice Mindful Gratitude: During daily activities, pause to notice and appreciate the small joys around you, such as the taste of a good meal or the sound of birds singing.

Use Gratitude Prompts: Questions like *"What made me smile today?"* or *"Who am I thankful for in my life?"* can help you focus on the positive.

Help Others Cultivate Gratitude: Share the tools and benefits you've gained from living in an *Attitude of Gratitude*. By inspiring others through your actions and conversations, you'll reinforce your own practice while fostering a deeper sense of self-worth. Helping others embrace gratitude enriches both their lives and your own.

Evening Reflections: If you can't clear concerning thoughts from your mind, writing in a journal before bed can be especially helpful. Take a moment to think about the good things that happened during your day, the gifts bestowed upon you and your loved ones today. Invite the universe to provide you with deep, restorative sleep, waking you in the morning with a feeling of refreshment and gratitude for a new day.

By intentionally asking for this, you're using the power of affirmations, which helps to manifest a peaceful, restful night and a renewed sense of positivity for tomorrow.

Over time, gratitude becomes second nature, transforming not just how you feel but how you experience the world. The more you practice, the more you'll find that gratitude isn't just a reaction to positive events—it becomes a proactive way of engaging with life.

Do you believe that cultivating gratitude as a daily practice can open your heart to more joy and transform the way you experience life?_____

If so, write down which of these practices you feel you can incorporate into your life, and include details about when and where you'll do them. The more detailed you are, the better, as this process helps create consistency and reinforces positive change.

_____

_____

_____

_____

_____

GRATITUDE IN CHALLENGING TIMES

Practicing gratitude during difficult periods may seem counterintuitive, but it is often when it benefits us most. Gratitude helps us find meaning and strength in adversity, shifting our focus from what we've lost to what remains. Here are some practices that may not take away the real pain, but can offer tools to help you process and cultivate gratitude with more balance in difficult situations:

Find Small Blessings: Even in hardship, there are moments of light. Look for small things to appreciate, such as a kind word or a moment of peace.

Shift Your Perspective: Ask yourself, *"What can I learn from this experience?"* or *"How can this challenge help me grow?"*

Keep a Gratitude Anchor: Identify something constant in your life that you can always be thankful for, such as a supportive friend or a cherished memory.

Focus on Inner Strength: Reflect on past challenges you've overcome and the strengths you gained from them.

Practicing gratitude during difficult times helps shift focus from loss to strength, allowing us to find courage, meaning, and small moments of light even in adversity.

Have you struggled to feel grateful during difficult times? _____

If so, write about a recent example where shifting into gratitude could have helped you find strength or ease your pain.

_____

_____

_____

_____

THE CONNECTION BETWEEN GRATITUDE & MANIFESTATION

Gratitude is a powerful force in the in the manifestation process. When you focus on what you are thankful for, you send a message to the universe that you are open to receiving more abundance. This aligns your energy with your desires, making them more likely to materialize.

Here are ways to incorporate gratitude into your manifestation practice:

Visualize Your Desires with Gratitude: Imagine your goals as already achieved and feel genuine gratitude for them.

Express Gratitude for the Journey: Appreciate the steps and lessons along the way, even before reaching your destination.

Combine Affirmations with Gratitude: Statements like *"I am so grateful for the opportunities coming my way"* amplify your intentions.

Gratitude and manifestation work in a loop: the more you appreciate, the more you attract—and the more you attract, the easier it becomes to appreciate.

Do you believe that gratitude helps align your energy with your desires, amplifying your ability to manifest them? _____

If so, write down one thing you're grateful for that aligns with something you wish to manifest, and one action you can add to your daily routine to bring more gratitude to that area, helping you manifest more powerfully.

_____

_____

_____

_____

INSPIRING STORIES OF GRATITUDE

The Survivor's Perspective: A cancer survivor shared how practicing gratitude during treatment allowed her to focus on the love and support of her family and the appreciation of her body. This shift in outlook not only gave her strength but also inspired and uplifted her loved ones during her recovery.

The Entrepreneur's Journey: A struggling entrepreneur began keeping a *Gratitude Journal*, which shifted his focus from financial stress to the small wins and supportive relationships in his life. This change in perspective helped him persevere and ultimately achieve greater success, not only in his business, but also in his relationships.

Gratitude in School: A teacher started a classroom tradition where students shared one thing they were grateful for each day. This practice not only boosted morale but also created a positive and supportive learning environment.

Gratitude at the Dinner Table: A family established a nightly tradition where each member shared their "low and high" of the day during dinner. This fostered connection by allowing everyone to express challenges while ending with gratitude. Over time, it became a cherished ritual that deepened bonds and encouraged positivity.

Do any of these stories of gratitude resonate with you? _____

If so, write about how that story speaks to you and why.

_____
_____
_____
_____
_____

GRATITUDE AS A LIFELONG PRACTICE

Gratitude isn't just a one-time activity—it's a habit that requires consistency and effort, but the rewards are immeasurable. Over time, practicing gratitude reshapes your perspective, strengthens your relationships, and brings more joy and abundance into your life.

There will be days, weeks, or even seasons when gratitude feels effortless, and others when it feels nearly impossible. Life's challenges can cloud our ability to see the good, and in those moments, it's easy to drift away from gratitude without realizing it. But *the goal isn't perfection—it's persistence.*

What matters most is recognizing it when we realize we are no longer living in the *Attitude of Gratitude* and making the choice to be grateful again. Even the smallest act of gratitude—a deep breath, a single acknowledgment of something good—can shift our perspective and reignite our joy.

Gratitude attracts life's goodness like a magnet, drawing more positive experiences and opportunities your way. But even when you struggle to feel grateful, know that simply trying is enough. Every time you return to gratitude, you strengthen your ability to find peace, joy, and abundance—no matter what life brings.

Do you prefer being around people who radiate gratitude versus those who focus on who or what's wrong in their life? _____

If so, write how being around both of those types of people affects your life and influences your outlook.

_____

_____

_____

_____

FOLLOWING YOUR GRATITUDE COMPASS

Gratitude is more than a feeling; it is a way of living that guides you toward what truly matters, inviting more of it into your life.

By making gratitude your compass, you can navigate life's challenges with grace while embracing its blessings with open arms. Even in the face of uncertainty, gratitude has the power to ground you, reminding you that light exists even on the darkest days.

Trust that every moment of appreciation strengthens your path forward, opening doors to unexpected joy and opportunities. Remember, the more you focus on gratitude, the more you will find to be grateful for. Let it lead you to a life of greater joy, connection, and abundance.

And whether life seems to be pulling you north, south, east, or west, gratitude grounds you, guiding you toward joy, clarity, and the path meant for you. If you ever feel lost, just remember to pull out your gratitude compass—it will always point you back in the right direction. No matter how far you stray, you can always return—by simply focusing on what you appreciate in this moment.

Can you imagine having an actual gratitude compass in your pocket, something you can reach for and look at whenever you need direction, especially in times of discomfort? _____

If so, think of one thing you'd like to change in your life and write down how using your gratitude compass could help you manifest that change.

_____

_____

_____

Perceptual Shifting in Relationships
PLAYING WELL WITH OTHERS

There was once a boy who lived in a home that echoed with laughter during the day and with silence—or shouting—at night.

His father loved him deeply. He told him he was brilliant, creative, destined for something great. They built forts, painted murals, and laughed until their ribs ached. His father told stories of knights, courage, and of filling the world with light.

But when he drank, something shifted. His eyes hardened. His voice changed. The man became unpredictable—sometimes cruel, sometimes violent. And though he never remembered the nights clearly, the bruises and broken things told their own version of the truth.

The next morning, his father would sob. He'd fall to his knees, kiss the boy's hands, and whisper apologies through tears. And the boy would believe him. Of course he would—he loved his father too. And in some strange way, he still felt like a hero.

But the boy grew up with two mirrors inside him—one that said, "You can do anything," and one that whispered, "You are nothing One that said, *"You can do anything."*

As he became a man, he swore he would never become like his father. And he didn't—not in the ways that mattered most. He quit drinking before having children. He never hit them. His kids never saw their father stumble, or rage, or cry apologies through a closed door.

They grew up with love. With safety. With belief in themselves.

But still, the man struggled. Relationships were confusing terrain. Trust came slowly. Vulnerability felt foreign. He longed to be loved so deeply that he failed to set boundaries. He built walls to protect himself—pushing away those he loved most, for fear of being hurt.

Without realizing it, he passed some of this confusion on to his children—sometimes through his actions, more often through his unhealed wounds. His inner battles left traces, as all unspoken pain does. He had done so much to break the cycle. And the cycle was broken.

But so was he.

Relationships are where our deepest patterns hide. *Even the strongest love can carry shadows.*

Still, there was hope.

Because one day, he realized *healing doesn't end with the promise to never become that which hurt us.* It continues with the willingness to become more—more aware, more open, more present.

He began the work not just of loving others, but of *loving himself. This was his greatest challenge.* Not just protecting his children, but helping them recognize the patterns of his past—so they could heal from the ghosts that had followed him into fatherhood.

And that is how change grows:

Not always in one generation, but across many.
In men who break cycles.
In women who forgive themselves.
In children who learn that what we see is not always the whole story—
and that love, at its truest, begins with opening everything up to others, even the wounds of silent wars.

Relationships are at the heart of the human experience, shaping our joy, growth, and sense of belonging. However, they are also complex and often

PERCEPTUAL SHIFTING IN RELATIONSHIPS

fraught with misunderstandings, conflicts, and emotional barriers. At the core of these challenges lies perception—the way we see and interpret others' words, actions, and intentions.

Perceptual Shifting is a powerful tool for transforming relationships. By changing how we view others and ourselves, we can break through barriers, deepen connections, and create relationships that are grounded in empathy, trust, and understanding. These shifts influence every interaction, from our closest bonds to our professional collaborations.

This chapter explores how to identify and shift perceptions in relationships, practical strategies for fostering connection, and the profound impact of seeing others through a lens of compassion and openness.

By practicing the art of living in the shift—and sustaining those shifts over time—you'll create healthier, more fulfilling relationships, many of which will last a lifetime

Would you say that having healthy relationships with others is an important goal for you? _____

If so, list a few of the most important people in your life with whom you'd like to strengthen your relationship, and consider how simply shifting the way you interact with them could improve your connection.

_____

_____

_____

_____

_____

_____

THE PERCEPTUAL SHIFT

FOUNDATIONAL PRINCIPLES OF LIVING IN THE SHIFT

The quality of your relationships is deeply influenced by the way you perceive and interpret interactions. These three core principles guide how we navigate and transform perspectives, ultimately leading to healthier and more fulfilling connections:

Awareness: Begin by acknowledging the lens you typically view relationships through. The more honest and self-aware you are at this stage, the greater the potential you have to improve your relationships. Are there patterns of blame, judgment, or insecurity that cloud your perspective?

Intentionality: Choose to improve your relationships by adjusting your behavior. Embrace curiosity and compassion, accepting that others may not change, and focus on shifting your response to create a more positive dynamic. This sets the stage for continuous *Perceptual Shifts*.

Practice: Relationships are constantly shifting, requiring consistent effort and applying new perspectives even when old habits resurface. *Growth isn't always linear*, but each time you choose to see with more understanding, patience, and love, you strengthen the foundation of your relationships.

By consistently choosing awareness, intentionality, and practice, you build a solid foundation for deeper, more fulfilling relationships that thrive on understanding, growth, and connection.

Do you think you can accept someone as they are, without expecting change, and still have a healthy relationship? _____

If so, write about someone you've wanted to change and how accepting them could improve your relationship, even if letting go is needed.

_____

_____

_____

HOW PERCEPTION AFFECTS RELATIONSHIPS

Every interaction we have is filtered through our personal perceptions. These perceptions are shaped by past experiences, beliefs, and emotional states.

Understanding that your perception is not the absolute truth, but one interpretation among many, is the first step in transforming how you relate to others. This awareness opens the door to curiosity, empathy, and meaningful change.

Cultural or societal norms can influence how we interpret roles, responsibilities, and expectations in relationships. Similarly, if you've been hurt in a previous relationship—and who hasn't—you might perceive a partner's actions as untrustworthy, even when they have good intentions.

Awareness of these patterns is the key that unlocks the opportunity to shift— to see situations with fresh eyes and to foster greater understanding and trust in your connections.

Do you understand how the concepts of perspective, expectations, and perceptions relate to each other? _____

If so, write about how shifting one or more of these could positively impact your relationships.

_____

_____

_____

_____

_____

_____

_____

COMMON PERCEPTUAL BARRIERS IN RELATIONSHIPS

Our perceptions shape how we interpret and respond to those around us, but sometimes these perceptions create unnecessary obstacles to connection and understanding. Some common red flags to watch for that can sabotage your relationships include:

Assumptions: Jumping to conclusions about someone's thoughts, feelings, or intentions can lead to misunderstandings and conflict.

Projection: Attributing your own *fears, insecurities, or desires* to someone else can distort your perception of their actions.

Negativity Bias: *Focusing on the negative* aspects of a relationship while *overlooking the positive* can erode trust and connection.

Fixed Narratives: Holding onto *rigid beliefs* about who someone is or how they behave *prevents growth and transformation.*

Perceptual Shifting allows us to challenge assumptions, release projections, and shift our focus from negativity to growth and connection. By cultivating empathy, curiosity, and openness, we transform not just how we see others but how we engage, listen, and build deeper, more fulfilling relationships.

Do you recognize how assumptions, projections, negative biases, and fixed narratives can sabotage relationships? _____

If so, write about a relationship where these patterns sometimes play a role and reflect on how you might change your approach.

_____

_____

_____

_____

STRATEGIES FOR INTEGRATING PERCEPTUAL SHIFTS IN RELATIONSHIPS

Integrating *Perceptual Shifts* in relationships takes effort and a commitment to deeper understanding, empathy, and open communication. Here are some ways to achieve it:

Practice Active Listening: Engaging with the intent to understand, rather than just to respond, allows you to fully absorb the other person's perspective. This approach fosters deeper connection and minimizes misunderstandings.

One effective strategy is to ask if they'd be comfortable with you taking notes during the discussion. This practice not only demonstrates your commitment to truly listening but also helps you absorb their insights without reacting defensively. By giving yourself time to reflect on their perceptions, you reinforce your dedication to self-improvement and build trust in the relationship.

Focus on Shared Goals: Shift your perspective from *"me versus you"* to *"us versus the problem."* Working collaboratively to identify and achieve mutual goals fosters trust, partnership, and mutual respect, strengthening the relationship and paving the way for shared success.

Cultivate Empathy: Put yourself in the other person's shoes. Literally imagine being them, in their physical body, with their issues, feelings and responsibilities. Consider how their life experiences and emotions have shaped their actions and choices.

Be Open to Constructive Feedback: When someone shares their perspective about your behavior, choices, or actions, it's easy to perceive it as criticism or an attempt to change you. Instead of reacting defensively or dismissing their words outright, take a moment to pause and consider whether there's any truth to their perception. From their view, could their feelings and requests hold a seed of validity?

Approaching these moments with curiosity and openness fosters self-reflection and growth. While honoring your feelings and not becoming a doormat, embracing change strengthens relationships and deepens self-awareness. Letting go of ego-driven defensiveness creates space for healthier, happier connections.

Speaking From the Heart: One of the most powerful ways to foster understanding and resolve conflict is by speaking from the heart. On my bathroom counter, I keep a childhood photo of myself—Jamie. Each morning, I kiss it, say I love you, and promise a fun moment that day. This simple ritual has deepened my self-love and understanding.

One day, I had a heated disagreement with Claire, whom I love deeply and who speaks the language of my heart. She asked me how Jamie felt. I stopped, thought about it, and said, "He's scared, hurt, upset, and confused." She replied that the little girl inside her felt the same. We hugged, and the disagreement dissolved.

This experience taught me the profound impact of setting aside blame and simply listening to each other's emotions. "Getting to the heart of the matter" is not just a phrase; it's a practice that can dissolve conflict and nurture connection.

Gratitude strengthens bonds and shifts your focus to the positive aspects of the relationship. Make it a habit to acknowledge what you value in others.

Do you recognize the importance of active listening, empathy, shared goals, and openness in improving relationships? _____

If so, reflect on which of these areas you could improve in your relationships, and how focusing on them could make your connections healthier and more fulfilling.

_____

_____

_____

_____

SHIFTING AND VULNERABILITY

Living in the Shift in relationships requires vulnerability. Being open about your thoughts, feelings, and desires allows for deeper connections. Vulnerability might feel uncomfortable, but it is the foundation of trust and intimacy.

Share Your Shifts: Talk openly with loved ones about your efforts to see things differently. This invites understanding and support. It's okay—and often understandable—if they're doubtful that you'll actually shift.

This work isn't about trying to get others to change, agree with, or support your efforts to grow. It's about shifting yourself into a place of compassion, empathy, and understanding. By doing so, you'll not only improve your relationships but also invite abundance into your life, filling you with greater happiness and peace.

Own Your Mistakes: Admitting when you've fallen back into old patterns, first to yourself and then to others if you've caused them any pain, demonstrates accountability and fosters mutual growth.

The ability to say, *"I recognize that my behavior isn't in line with the person I want to be. You don't deserve to be treated that way, and I'll strive to do better next time,"* shows a genuine effort to grow. It prevents them from having unrealistic expectations by acknowledging that perfection isn't possible. You'll do your best—that's all anyone can ask of you.

However, if your honesty and vulnerability is met with criticism or abuse, it's important to set boundaries and detach with love. Owning your mistakes should create intimacy, not open the door to abuse.

Ask for Feedback: Invite others to share their perspectives on your efforts to shift, approaching the conversation with an open mind and a genuine desire to grow. If you sense criticism or blame, focus on making the other person feel heard and understood.

Living in the Shift within relationships means embracing vulnerability, accountability, and a willingness to grow. It's about shifting your own perspective toward compassion and understanding while fostering deeper connections.

You create opportunities for trust and intimacy, paving the way for healthier and more fulfilling relationships, when we:

- *Own your mistakes, making verbal and living amends,*
- *Set healthy boundaries, following through with the consequences, and*
- *Share your efforts openly, speaking from the heart.*

By committing to these practices, you cultivate relationships rooted in authenticity, mutual respect, and lasting connection.

Do you believe that vulnerability in relationships is important and that it fosters deeper connections? _____

If so, which of these areas are you consistent with—taking responsibility for your mistakes, making amends, setting boundaries with consequences, or communicating with compassion from the heart—and which do you need to work on most?

_____
_____
_____
_____
_____
_____
_____

NAVIGATING CONFLICTS WITH OTHERS

Here are some ways to shift your perceptions with challenging people:

Pause and Reflect: When conflict arises—often triggered by discomfort or the fear of it—pause before reacting. Consider whether past experiences or assumptions are shaping your perception.

Seek Understanding: Approach situations with curiosity, asking questions to understand the other person's perspective. Focus on discernment, which observes and seeks clarity, rather than judgment, which divides and criticizes.

Reframe the Narrative: Replace negative or limiting beliefs with more empowering ones. For example, instead of thinking, *"They don't care about me,"* try, *"They might be struggling with something I don't know about."*

Practice Compassion: Put yourself in the other person's shoes. Consider how their experiences and emotions—both past and present— might be influencing their words and actions.

Communicate Openly: Share your thoughts honestly and invite the other person to do the same. If they're not ready, don't take it personally. Instead, listen with an open heart to foster understanding and resolution.

Navigating conflict with awareness, compassion, and open communication fosters deeper understanding, strengthens relationships, and paves the way for meaningful resolution.

Do you think that these tools aid in healthy communication? _____

Which practice could you improve on, and with whom could it be most useful?

_____
_____
_____
_____

PERCEPTUAL SHIFTING WITH THE FAMILY

Family dynamics are often influenced by deep-seated patterns and roles. Shifting perceptions in these relationships can lead to healing, understanding, and renewed connection. Strategies for changing the way we see things in families include:

Letting Go of Labels: Avoid labeling family members based on past behaviors. Allow them the space to grow and change.

Focusing on Intentions: Recognize that family members' actions, even when misguided, often stem from a desire to heal, help or connect.

Creating More Intimacy: Shift family dynamics by introducing new ways of interacting, such as regular family check-ins or shared activities.

Setting Healthy Boundaries: Knowing what's acceptable and what's not regarding how others treat you is essential for maintaining respect and harmony in any relationship, particularly in families. Shifting your perception to see boundaries as acts of self-care, rather than rejection, can make them easier to implement. You'll learn more about setting and honoring boundaries in the upcoming section, *How to Shift in Challenging Relationships*.

What's important to remember is that by actively and intentionally practicing *Perceptual Shifting* with our family members, we create space for growth, deeper understanding, and more meaningful connections built on mutual respect and love.

Do you find it difficult to know when to set boundaries with others and when to let go of certain issues? _____

If so, write the name of one person you trust, who has healthy relationships, that you could run boundary-setting decisions by.

SHIFTING PERCEPTION IN ROMANTIC RELATIONSHIPS

Romantic relationships are deeply rewarding but often require ongoing effort to navigate differences and maintain connection. *Perceptual Shifting* can help couples move from conflict to collaboration and from disconnection to intimacy. Here's how:

Challenge Unrealistic Expectations: Many conflicts arise from unspoken or unrealistic expectations. By discussing and recalibrating your expectations together, you create a foundation of intimacy and mutual understanding.

When both partners clearly express what they need—and what they can realistically give—misunderstandings and resentments fade. This collaborative approach not only strengthens the relationship but also fosters trust, as both partners feel heard, valued, and respected.

Celebrate Differences: Instead of seeing differences as obstacles, view them as opportunities to learn from each other and grow together.

In *The Attitudes of Gratitude in Love*, M.J. Ryan shares the story of a woman growing increasingly frustrated with her husband's slow pace, feeling it was driving her crazy. Realizing her frustration was putting their marriage at risk, she embraced a *Perceptual Shift*. Instead of seeing his slowness as a flaw, she reframed it as equanimity—and began to view him as her live-in Buddha, helping her find calm and balance.

Revisit the Positive: Reflect on the qualities and moments that drew you to your partner. Gratitude and appreciation can shift your focus from criticism to connection.

Reframe Conflict: Rather than seeing disagreements as personal attacks, view them as opportunities to address issues and strengthen your bond. When approached with openness and curiosity, conflicts can become stepping stones toward deeper understanding and greater connection in the relationship.

Perceptual Shifting in romantic relationships fosters deeper connection, perseverance in the face of adversity, and mutual growth. By challenging unrealistic expectations, embracing differences, and reframing conflict, couples can cultivate stronger, more fulfilling partnerships.

It's important to remember that both of you ultimately want the same thing—a deeper, more fulfilling love. When approached with openness and curiosity, challenges become opportunities to strengthen your bond rather than divide you. Through gratitude, communication, and a willingness to shift perspectives, relationships can evolve into a dynamic space of trust, intimacy, and shared growth.

Do you find that unrealistic expectations or misunderstandings often cause tension in your relationships? _____

If so, think about a recent conflict and write down the situation.

_____

_____

_____

_____

What might have happened if you had paused before communicating and reflected on any expectations you had going into the conversation?

_____

_____

_____

_____

Could you have asked for more clarification before diving in? _____

PERCEPTUAL SHIFTING IN BUSINESS

Workplace relationships can be challenging due to differing communication styles, goals, and hierarchies. *Perceptual Shifting* fosters empathy, improves communication, and promotes mutual respect. Here are ways to shift your perspective at work in order to get the most from your job and colleagues:

Assume Positive Intent: Start with the belief that coworkers are doing their best, even if their approach differs from yours.

Value Diversity: Recognize that diverse perspectives can lead to innovative solutions. Shift your perception to see differences as strengths, knowing that varied perspectives create successful collaborations.

Address Misunderstandings Promptly: Rather than letting resentment build, approach misunderstandings with a calm, open mind. Seek to understand the other person's perspective first and find common ground in a respectful and constructive way.

Focus on Shared Goals: Reframe conflicts as opportunities to align on common objectives, improve workflow, and uncover valuable opportunities for creativity, growth, and productivity.

By focusing on shared goals, appreciating individual contributions, and addressing disparities with openness and fairness, teams can create an environment where everyone feels valued and motivated to give their best.

Do you ever experience relationship challenges with others at work, even if you work from home? _____

If so, think about a recent issue. What tools from the strategies above could you bring more consistently to the table to improve communication and collaboration?

_____

_____

SHIFTING PERCEPTIONS IN CHALLENGING RELATIONSHIPS

You've seen these concepts before—and that's on purpose. Mastery comes from practice, not just reading. Repetition is how we shift from knowing to living. Each time you revisit a tool from a new angle, you deepen your understanding and expand your ability to apply it in real life.

Not all relationships are easy, and some can be especially challenging. *Perceptual Shifts* can provide the tools to navigate these dynamics with greater ease and clarity. Here's how:

Set Boundaries: Recognize that shifting your perspective doesn't mean tolerating harmful behavior or compromising your well-being. Healthy boundaries aren't about controlling others or demanding that they change their behavior. Instead, they're about clearly communicating what makes you uncomfortable and how you'll take care of yourself if those behaviors persist.

When you set a boundary, you're not imposing rules or limits on others; instead, you're defining the actions you'll take to maintain an *Attitude of Gratitude* and protect your emotional and mental well-being. For example, if someone crosses a boundary, reasserting it repeatedly is less effective than following through on the consequences you previously communicated, such as stepping away or disengaging.

This approach helps you maintain your integrity, prioritize self-care, and handle challenges with grace and respect for both yourself and others. It also sends a clear message that you mean what you say—discouraging repeated boundary violations and reinforcing the importance of mutual respect in maintaining a healthy relationship.

Focus on the Lesson: Difficult relationships often hold valuable lessons that can lead to profound personal growth. Instead of dwelling on the pain or frustration, ask yourself, *"What have I learned from this experience?"*

Consider how the situation can help you cultivate qualities like patience, empathy, equanimity, or improved communication skills.

If you slip up and react impulsively instead of pausing, use the experience as a learning opportunity. Reflect on it in your journal, focusing on areas for growth and reframing challenges in a positive light. When your words, actions, or inactions have caused harm, take responsibility and make amends to repair the relationship.

By identifying the lessons and recording your progress, you create a powerful narrative of transformation that not only helps you move forward but also equips you to approach future relationships with greater wisdom and understanding. It also shows the other person that you value the relationship enough to make a sincere effort to change, while setting an example of *Perceptual Shifting* that they may be inspired to emulate.

Release Expectations: Let go of the desire for others to change, as holding onto this expectation often keeps you trapped in a cycle of blame and victimhood. This habit is one of the most common patterns in dysfunctional relationships.

When you focus on what others should do differently, you surrender your power to create positive change in your own life. This mindset can leave you feeling frustrated, helpless, and stuck, as it relies on external factors that are beyond your control. Instead, shift your focus inward—on your own growth, healing, and the ways you can respond differently to challenging situations.

It's natural to feel like someone else's behavior should change, especially when it's causing harm or frustration. This thinking is understandable, and it's important to acknowledge that desire. However, the reality is that we don't have the power to force someone else to change. The opportunity here is not about controlling others but about reclaiming your own peace and happiness through *Perceptual Shifting*. By focusing on your personal growth, you can create a better reality for yourself, regardless of whether they change or not.

By releasing expectations and taking responsibility for your actions and mindset, you break free from the blame cycle, reclaim your sense of empowerment, and cultivate healthier, more authentic relationships. This shift doesn't mean you condone harmful behavior, it means you're prioritizing your well-being while allowing others the space to grow—or not—on their terms.

Use your journal to explore these shifts, reflecting on where expectations might be holding you back and how embracing your own growth can lead to transformative outcomes. Releasing expectations doesn't just benefit you—it sets an example of personal accountability that others may be inspired to follow, fostering a healthier dynamic in your relationships.

Detach with Love: Detaching with love doesn't necessarily mean leaving the person or ending the relationship altogether—though there are times when stepping away completely is the healthiest choice. It's about creating emotional space to protect your well-being while maintaining compassion and respect for *both* yourself and the other person.

Detachment allows you to break free from cycles of unhealthy interactions, setting boundaries that preserve your peace without harboring resentment or blame. There will be moments when detaching with love feels nearly impossible, especially in the heat of intense emotions. Pause. During those times, take a deep, slow breath. Remind yourself that even if you can't detach with love, it's still important to detach.

Aim to step back without anger or malice. Reacting impulsively—such as hanging up the phone abruptly or walking away mid-argument—can escalate tension and leave you feeling worse later. Instead, focus on pausing before you say or do something that could "mess up your side of the street." If the interaction is unhealthy, communicate your intent to detach, calmly and respectfully, such as saying, *"I'm going to take a moment to cool down before we continue."* Then do it.

There may be times when your decision to detach is met with resistance. The other person might even try to make you feel guilty for "abandoning" them. In such cases, you can reassure them by saying something like, *"I'm not abandoning you or the relationship. I just don't feel well and need a break, then I'll be back,"* while still maintaining your boundary.

When detachment feels difficult or painful, reflect on your experience in your journal. Writing can help you process your emotions, uncover patterns, and clarify how you can detach in a way that supports your mental and emotional health. If you've done a good job at detaching, then celebrate that as a victory.

Ultimately, detaching with love is about prioritizing your peace while leaving the door open for healing, whether within the relationship or in yourself. Detaching with love is a balancing act. Learning to set and enforce healthy boundaries takes time and practice. Avoid being overly rigid—sometimes referred to as a "drama queen or king"—by using boundaries at the slightest hint of a problem, but don't become a doormat either.

Healthy communication requires effort as well, and while this new way of interacting might feel unfamiliar or uncomfortable at first, stick with it! Over time and with consistency, it will become second nature.

Do you recognize that many of the tools discussed earlier in this book, like setting boundaries, releasing expectations, and detaching with love, are repeated here to help you navigate challenging relationships? _____

If so, write about why you think it's important to revisit these tools and apply them in these situations. (I'm asking you to put these concepts into your own words because the more you use that pen to internalize this information, the higher the likelihood you'll start using it in all your relationships, and your life will take off like a rocketship.)

_____

_____

_____

_____

_____

_____

PRACTICAL EXERCISES FOR PERCEPTUAL SHIFTS IN RELATIONSHIPS

Strengthening relationships requires intentional effort and a willingness to see things from a new perspective. These practical exercises will help you foster deeper, more meaningful connections.

The Gratitude Letter: Take a moment to set aside any challenges in your relationship and focus on the positive. Write a letter, text, or email expressing appreciation for the person's positive qualities and the impact they've had on your life. Share it with them if you feel comfortable.

Role Reversal: Imagine yourself in the other person's shoes. How might they view the situation? What emotions might they be experiencing? This practice fosters compassion and empathy, helping you understand their perspective and the reasons behind their behavior.

The Assumption Audit: Reflect on a recent conflict. Identify any assumptions you made and consider alternative explanations for the other person's behavior. Explore whether your preconceived ideas or biases might be influencing your interactions.

Active Listening Practice: In your next conversation, listen fully without interrupting. Summarize the other person's thoughts to show you've heard them. If a response is needed, it's often helpful to give the conversation some space and ask for time to reflect, process, and revisit it later.

By integrating *Perceptual Shifting* exercises into your daily interactions, you can reduce conflict and build stronger, more fulfilling relationships.

Can you see how you might benefit from practicing the exercises above in your relationships? _____

If so, choose one from above, stop reading and practice it right now. Write down which exercise you used.

SUSTAINING PERCEPTUAL SHIFTS OVER TIME

Continuing the practice of shifting in relationships requires commitment to personal growth and consistent adaptation. The following practices will help nurture the positive changes you've made so far:

Daily Reflection: Spend a few minutes each day reflecting on your interactions. Celebrate moments where you embodied your new perspective and identify areas for improvement.

Mindfulness: Stay present in your interactions. Notice when old patterns arise and gently redirect yourself to your new perspective. This practice helps you stay grounded and respond with intention, rather than reverting to automatic reactions.

Accountability Partnerships: Share your goals with a trusted friend or mentor who can support and encourage you. Having someone to check in with not only helps you stay on track, but also offers a fresh perspective and accountability to reinforce your commitment to growth.

Celebrate Progress: Acknowledge the positive changes in your relationships as a result of your efforts. This reinforces your commitment to *Living in the Shift*.

Sustaining *Perceptual Shifts* in relationships requires consistency, mindfulness, and support. Reflecting daily, staying present, and celebrating progress strengthens your commitment to evolving into your best self.

Do you see consistency as a challenge when trying to implement new behaviors in your life and relationships? _____

If so, pause and set two daily calendar reminders on your phone—one at 10 AM, one at 5 PM—with two alerts each. Label them: "Shift NOW into love, compassion, kindness, and gratitude." Let these serve as gentle nudges toward your new way of being.

Check this box once completed: ☐

INSPIRING STORIES OF RELATIONSHIPS TRANSFORMATION

A Couple: A couple on the brink of divorce saved their relationship by shifting their focus from blame to shared responsibility. By learning to communicate from the heart, practicing empathy and gratitude, they rekindled their connection and created a stronger environment.

A Friendship: Two longtime friends who had grown apart reconnected by shifting their focus from past grievances to shared values and memories. Through honest conversations and mutual forgiveness, they rebuilt their bond.

A Father & Daughter: A father and daughter who hadn't spoken for years rebuilt their relationship by shifting their perceptions of each other's past actions. Through open dialogue, they found understanding and forgiveness.

The Workplace: A manager and employee with conflicting styles learned to appreciate each other's strengths by focusing on shared goals. This shift led to improved communication and a more productive partnership.

These stories all share a common theme of transforming relationships by shifting perceptions, focusing on understanding, and fostering open communication. In each case, the individuals involved moved away from blame, past grievances, or differences, and instead embraced empathy, shared values, or mutual goals to rebuild trust, connection, and collaboration. Whether in romantic relationships, friendships, family dynamics, or the workplace, these shifts created space for growth, healing, and stronger, more fulfilling connections.

Can you see how practicing these new behaviors could create abundance in all your relationships? _____

If so, write down which relationship in your life right now would benefit most from your practice of perceptually shifting.

HOW SHIFTING IN RELATIONSHIPS CREATE OUTWARD RIPPLES

When you live the shift in relationships, the impact extends beyond the immediate connection. Your shifts plant seeds of compassion in others, inspiring them to grow.

Modeling Growth: Once others begin to recognize that you're *Perceptual Shifting* in a way that makes you more pleasant and approachable, as well as creating more abundance, they may be encouraged to learn how to do it themselves. This can create a ripple effect of growth and positive change within your relationships.

Fostering Community: *Perceptual Shifting can be contagious*, spreading throughout a community and guiding people toward love, understanding, joy, and balance. When others see the positive impact of responding with kindness and compassion, it inspires them to adopt the same mindset. This creates a ripple effect where everyone thrives in an environment rooted in mutual respect and connection. As each person shifts, the collective energy becomes one of growth and harmony, benefiting the entire community.

Creating Generational Change: *Perceptual Shifters* are more intuitive, less impulsive, and deeply compassionate. By modeling healthy dynamics, they manifest abundance through kindness and love—encouraging future generations to value connection and understanding. My children grew up hearing me say, "I love my life!"—a simple affirmation that helped shape a legacy of positivity. Now I see them embracing gratitude and joy in their own lives, and I can't help but believe I played some small part in their ability to love life so fully.

Is helping others find joy and peace important to you? _____

If so, who would benefit most from your example of joy and peace?

_____

_____

ENLIGHTENED PERSPECTIVES CREATE DEEPER CONNECTIONS

Living in the Shift in relationships is a journey of growth, connection, and transformation. It requires consistent effort and a commitment to shifting our perception from seeing others defensively to approaching them with empathy and curiosity. As you practice *Perceptual Shifting*, your relationships will become richer, more fulfilling, and more resilient.

The path to stronger relationships begins with a willingness to adopt a new perspective. Becoming good at this will help you transform not only your connections but also your own life, contributing to a more compassionate and connected world. Developing healthy communication skills is like learning a foreign language—it takes practice, patience, and persistence. Though it may involve growing pains, the journey is immensely rewarding.

Do your best, embrace the process, and view it as an opportunity to create deeper connections and a better version of yourself. The power to change your relationships begins with you, and the rewards are immeasurable.

Do you really think that adopting a new perspective by learning to positively Perceptually Shift in your relationships can actually create deeper connections and a more fulfilling life? _____

Can this shift guide you toward healthier relationships and away from toxic ones? _____

If so, name one specific relationship and describe the changes you'd like to see—then list the shifts you can make to support that transformation.

_____

_____

_____

_____

MANIFESTING ABUNDANCE

Reinventing Your Roadmap

RESHAPE YOUR FUTURE

There was once a remarkable young man. He was the kind of student parents and professors admire—brilliant, disciplined, and driven. By his final year of engineering school, he was at the top of his class. The degree, the job offers, the proud family—everything was lining up just as it was supposed to.

But as graduation approached, he began waking each day with a sick feeling in his stomach. He couldn't quite explain it. He'd always been good at engineering, and even liked it—so why now did it feel… empty? Hollow. Purposeless. Like a future borrowed from someone else. It no longer resonated with his heart.

Unsure of what to do, he called his uncle—someone who had spent decades walking his own unconventional path, guided more by intuition than expectation. He spoke quietly, afraid to disappoint the people who had always cheered him on. His uncle listened, then said gently:

"You have only one life to live—and it's yours. Be brave. Tell the truth. Follow your heart, no matter what it costs."

And so, he did.

After graduation, with barely any money to his name, he traveled to Naknek, Alaska, where he spent a summer canning salmon to earn a few thousand dollars. He invested some in the stock market and used the rest to begin a bold new chapter—solo-hiking the Appalachian Trail, the longest hiking-only footpath in the world, starting in Millinocket, Maine.
Alone with his thoughts for months, he grew stronger. Clearer. Wiser.

When his money ran out, he picked up jobs—working as a lifty at a ski lodge, a restaurant worker, a forestry technician cutting trees and battling wildfires. In between, he wandered. He saved. He invested. He explored.

Eventually, his modest investments grew enough to fund what he called his *"nomadic education."*

He biked down the Cape of Africa and across South Central Asia.
Through the sands of Saudi Arabia.
Ran for cover from lightning.
Felt the unexpected generosity of the Taliban in Afghanistan.
Yelled like a madman in the hills of Ethiopia.
Dodged bullets in Mexico.
Slept in a Sudanese jail.
Was chased in Kenya and Sudan.
Drank horse milk in a yurt with a Krgyzstan nomad.
Evaded police on a motorbike along death-defying cliffs in Pakistan.
Camped beside an erupting volcano.

And the years passed by—not in calendars or clocks, but in stories, scars, and starlit awakenings. Not in promotions or paychecks, but in encounters that cracked him open and stitched him back together.

Through it all, he discovered that **home isn't a place—it's a feeling**.
It's where people make you feel like you belong.

He witnessed hatred, ignorance, fear, and cruelty. But he also saw breathtaking love. Radical generosity. The quiet, unwavering humanity of strangers.

And what he came to understand is this:
Life isn't about hiding from the world's darkness.
It's about *seeing everything*—the beauty and the brutality—and still choosing love. Still choosing presence. Still choosing to say yes.
That choice begins, always, by loving and accepting yourself.

He slept under stars. Bathed in rivers. Wandered through deserts and across continents, all the while asking:

"What else is out there—and what else is within me?"

This isn't a fable.

This is a true story about my nephew, someone I love deeply—one of the most extraordinary individuals I've ever known. He didn't just create a new roadmap. He reminded me that the bravest path begins the moment we finally say:

"This life is mine."

Creating a new roadmap isn't about erasing the past—it's about using its lessons to chart a more fulfilling future. This process requires self-reflection, intentionality, and the courage to step outside your comfort zone. By the end of this chapter, you'll have the tools to design a life that inspires and empowers you.

Ask Yourself: Are you ready to plot a new, healthier course? Are you willing to release the past and embrace the possibility of a brighter future? Most importantly, do you have the courage to take this transformative step?

Are you ready to let go and start taking action? _____

If your answer is yes, great! You're ready to start shifting your perception—and loving your life in ways you may not have imagined. But before you can chart a new course, it's helpful to understand your starting point. Reflection helps you assess your current situation and identify what is and isn't working in your life. Here are a few powerful ways to take action.

Evaluate Key Areas of Your Life: Consider your career, relationships, finances, health, personal growth, and leisure. Could any or all of these areas of your life be improved? If so, here's some things to consider.

Identify Patterns: Reflect on recurring themes in your thoughts, beliefs, behaviors, and outcomes. Are there patterns that have held you back? Identify them and write them down.

Acknowledge Your Strengths and Challenges: Regularly celebrate your achievements and successful relationships, along with areas for improvement. This balanced perspective will inform your roadmap.

Understand and Clarify Your Values: Values represent what is most important to you in life—whether it's integrity, kindness, freedom, success, family, creativity, or personal growth. They act as your internal compass, helping you navigate choices and align your actions with your sense of purpose and identity. Understanding your values is essential because it:

- *Clarifies Your Priorities*: When you know what matters most to you, it becomes easier to prioritize your time, energy, and resources effectively.

- *Guides Decision-Making*: Values help you make choices that align with who you are and what you stand for, reducing inner conflict and regret.

- *Builds Authenticity*: Living in alignment with your values fosters a sense of authenticity, which strengthens self-confidence and self-respect.

- *Improves Relationships*: Knowing your values helps you establish healthy boundaries and connect with others whose values resonate with yours. It also encourages you to stay away from individuals whose values consistently clash with your own, helping you maintain healthier, more supportive relationships built on mutual respect and understanding.

- *Enhances Fulfillment*: Acting in alignment with your values creates a sense of purpose and satisfaction, as your actions reflect your true self.

By identifying and understanding where you're at now, and where you want to be, *you can live a more intentional and meaningful life, one that feels congruent with your authentic self.*

Are you ready to start balancing your life and moving toward healthier behaviors that will bring you greater happiness? _____

If so, on the following page, fill in the circle between each pair of traits that best represents where you are right now. When you reach the end of this book, come back here and see if anything has changed.

CREATING A NEW ROADMAP

SELF-REFLECTION INVENTORY

Self-Centered ———○○○○○○○○——— Empathetic

Jealous/Envious ———○○○○○○○○——— Grateful

Skeptical ———○○○○○○○○——— Optimistic

Critical ———○○○○○○○○——— Encouraging

Angry ———○○○○○○○○——— Happy

Anxious ———○○○○○○○○——— Calm

Fearful ———○○○○○○○○——— Confident

Frustrated ———○○○○○○○○——— Easy Going

Selfish ———○○○○○○○○——— Giving

Uncaring ———○○○○○○○○——— Loving

Closed Off ———○○○○○○○○——— Vulnerable

Procrastinating ———○○○○○○○○——— Industrious

ENVISIONING YOUR IDEAL LIFE

Envisioning your ideal life is a powerful first step toward creating a meaningful roadmap. Use these prompts to guide your vision:

Define success on your own terms, taking into account every aspect of your life. Clearly identify the feelings you wish to cultivate through your accomplishments and acquisitions, ensuring they align with your deeper sense of fulfillment.

What does success look like to you?

CREATING A NEW ROADMAP

Reflect on activities, people, and experiences that light you up.
How can you build on them and incorporate more of these into your life?

_____
_____
_____
_____
_____
_____
_____
_____
_____
_____

What brings you joy, even during difficult or uncertain times?

_____
_____
_____
_____
_____
_____

Transform Your Failures, Disappointments, and Mistakes: Life will inevitably include setbacks—it's part of being human. Your past holds vital clues for your future. Envision how you'd like to respond to these moments.

How can failures become lessons, disappointments become opportunities, and mistakes become stepping stones?

_____
_____
_____
_____
_____
_____
_____
_____
_____

Write down some examples from your life, reflecting on how you've grown or could grow from those experiences.

_____
_____
_____
_____
_____
_____

CREATING A NEW ROADMAP

Envision the best version of yourself. Knowing who you want to evolve into is one of the most empowering steps toward creating a life you love, as it provides a clear direction for your growth and transformation.

What qualities, habits, and achievements define this best version of you?

_____
_____
_____
_____
_____
_____
_____
_____

Who do you want to become?

_____
_____
_____
_____
_____
_____
_____
_____
_____
_____
_____

Reflect on the emotional, spiritual, and values-based impact you wish to have on others and the world, focusing on how you want to be remembered for the love, kindness, and principles you shared throughout your journey.

What legacy do you want to leave?

Walking through the past, especially the difficult experiences, is an important part of reflection. It allows you to identify patterns, recognize areas for growth, and imagine how you'd like to change moving forward. However, it's essential not to get stuck there.

Set a healthy boundary—spend no more than 15 minutes reflecting on past frustrations or mistakes. Then, shift your attention toward growth, gratitude, and the life you're actively creating.

This approach helps you find growth in each experience, while gently redirecting your energy toward who you're becoming. And ending the day in the *Attitude of Gratitude*—especially before coming home to family or loved ones—makes all the difference.

Know that it's natural to experience speed bumps and feelings of discomfort—*Perceptual Shifting* isn't about hiding or denying them. It's about recognizing them, pausing to consider different perspectives, and then consciously shifting out of them to return to a place of gratitude and joy.

Are you ready to envision a life shaped by integrity, kindness, growth, and connection? _____

If so, take a moment to reflect on what your life would look like if these values were at the core of everything you do. How would you like them to shape your relationships, career, and overall sense of fulfillment?

_____

_____

_____

_____

_____

_____

SETTING INTENTIONS AND GOALS

Once you've begun shifting your perspective, setting clear intentions and goals becomes a vital part of designing your new life roadmap. By reexamining how you perceive challenges, opportunities, and your own capabilities, you can approach goal-setting with a deeper sense of clarity and alignment.

This process isn't just about achieving milestones; it's about ensuring that your goals reflect the values and vision you've cultivated through your new practice of *Perceptual Shifting*.

Using the *SMART Framework*—Specific, Measurable, Achievable, Relevant, and Time-bound—you can design goals that are practical and aligned with your shifting mindset. This ensures your progress stays grounded in your evolving values and vision.

For example, reframe a vague desire like *"I want to be successful"* into a clearly defined and aligned goal: *"I will complete a professional certification in six months to advance my career while maintaining balance in my personal life."* This reframing incorporates clarity and purpose, which are hallmarks of *The Perceptual Shift*.

SMART FRAMEWORK FOR GOAL-SETTING

- **Specific**: Clearly define what you want to accomplish and why it matters to you in your evolving vision. Avoid generalizing.

- **Measurable**: Identify how you'll track progress, creating a feedback loop to celebrate small wins along the way. Journal Charts work great. You can see samples of these in *The Perceptual Shift Journal*.

- **Achievable**: Leverage your new perception of challenges as "growth opportunities" to ensure goals are within reach.

- **Relevant**: Align your goals with your evolving values and aspirations, ensuring they support your overall transformation.

- **Time-bound**: Set deadlines to maintain momentum, recognizing that timeframes help anchor your vision in actionable steps. Again, this can be incorporated into a Journal Chart.

Break Goals into Steps: Divide larger goals into smaller tasks that feel manageable, enabling steady progress while maintaining motivation. This approach makes *Perceptual Shifting* easier by shooting for incremental growth and embracing patience.

Prioritize with Clarity: Focus on goals that align with your deeper, more loving values and perceptions, ensuring they contribute meaningfully to your life. Avoid spreading yourself too thin, recognizing that fewer, well-aligned goals are more impactful.

Balance and Alignment: Align your goals with balanced values. This means ensuring they reflect not only your aspirations for an abundant life but also your commitment to self-care and service to others. This balance fosters long-term fulfillment and reinforces the broader *Perceptual Shift* you're working toward.

When approached through the lens of *Perceptual Shifting*, goal-setting is no longer just a task—it's a conscious reflection of who you're becoming. It transforms into a dynamic tool for designing a life filled with purpose, harmony, and abundance. By tying your goals to your evolving mindset, you ensure they guide you toward a life that truly reflects your highest self.

Do you feel ready to set goals that align with your new perspective and values? _____

If so, write down three realistic goals for the next year. Make sure they stretch you just enough to spark growth—without overwhelming your system.

_____

_____

_____

BUILDING A SUPPORT SYSTEM

Creating a new roadmap is easier when you have a strong support system. Surround yourself with people who inspire, encourage, and hold you accountable. Consider the following:

Identify Your Allies: *Who in your life uplifts you, supports your growth, and shares your core values?*

_____

_____

Lean on these individuals for guidance and encouragement. At the same time, consider gently stepping back from those who remain entrenched in a victim mindset and resist taking steps toward creating a life they love.

Seek Mentors: Find individuals who have achieved the mindset or goals you aspire to. Their insights can provide valuable guidance and inspire growth, especially if you embark on this journey together.

Join Communities: Connect with groups or networks, online or in person, that align with your goals. Engaging with these fosters a sense of belonging and shared purpose.

Communicate Your Vision: Share your roadmap with trusted friends or family members. Their feedback and support can help you stay on track.

Do you recognize the importance of having a strong support system as you create your new roadmap? _____

If so, list a few shared core values (such as respect, honesty, and compassion) that are important to you in building trust with your support system.

_____

_____

EMBRACING FLEXIBILITY

Life is unpredictable, and even the best-laid plans can encounter detours. Embracing flexibility empowers you to adapt to and even embrace change, all while remaining aligned with your vision. Here's how:

Revisit Your Roadmap Regularly: Take a moment to reflect on your journey—celebrate your progress, embrace the lessons learned, and reassess your goals with intention. Let your journal become a space where your evolving dreams and growth opportunities take shape. Life is ever-changing, and so should be your roadmap to fulfillment.

Stay Open to New Opportunities: Sometimes, unexpected paths lead to the most rewarding destinations. Choose to embrace uncertainty rather than fear, as these paths often hold possibilities you never imagined and could align perfectly with your evolving dreams.

Practice Bouncebackability: Cultivate a mindset that embraces change and sees challenges as catalysts for growth. Don't let setbacks get you down—use them to pull you up. Every obstacle is an opportunity to adapt, grow stronger, and build the confidence to face future challenges with grace.

Disappointments, unmet expectations, and *"shattered dreams,"* while painful, often hold hidden lessons. These experiences can offer insights that help lift you out of victimhood and into resilience and wisdom. Ask yourself, *"What can I gain from this?"* Writing down your reflections helps solidify these lessons, reinforcing the **Perceptual Shifts** you're incorporating into your life.

And remember to give yourself grace. While some challenges are serious, managing stress is key—find ways to lighten the load and stay balanced. Though it may feel difficult, try to lighten the moment—often humor can help restore balance.

Often, the *"worst"* things that happen turn out to be the *"best"* things that happen—we just need to give it time to understand why. Cultivate a mindset that embraces change and views detours as unexpected gifts. Remember, every setback is an opportunity to adapt, grow stronger, and build the confidence to face future obstacles with grace.

Embracing flexibility allows you to reinvent yourself, say *"yes"* to new opportunities, and turn challenges into stepping stones toward even greater abundance. By staying adaptable and open, you align with your vision and invite more growth, success, and fulfillment into your life.

Do you see the value of adapting to life's frequently unpredictable changes while staying aligned with your vision? ____

If so, reflect on a recent setback or detour. How can you embrace it as an opportunity for growth and use it to strengthen your resilience and confidence moving forward?

_____

_____

_____

_____

Write one or two ways you can apply what you've learned so far in this book to approach this challenge. How might these insights help you move forward into a solution and bring you peace of mind?

_____

_____

_____

_____

_____

PRACTICAL EXERCISES FOR CREATING YOUR ROADMAP

By using simple yet effective tools to visualize your aspirations and evaluate your current path, you'll set a clear direction for growth in emotional health, peace of mind, better relationships, and abundance. These practices guide you in defining your ideal life while creating space for reflection and accountability. Doing them in a group—or alongside others practicing *Perceptual Shifting*—is a great way to have fun with the process and receive valuable feedback.

The Vision Board: Create a visual representation of your ideal life with images, words, and symbols that inspire you. Place it where you'll see it daily to keep your goals in focus. Update it often to reflect your evolving vision. (Instructions for creating a vision board are later in the book).

The "Perfect Day" Exercise: Write a detailed description of your ideal day, from morning to night. This helps clarify what matters most to you. By vividly imagining your perfect day, you can gain deeper insight into your values and desires, making it easier to align your actions with your aspirations.

The Wheel of Life: Draw a circle and divide it into six sections, each representing a key area of your life: **Physical Health, Mental and Emotional Well-being, Relationships, Career/Purpose, Financial Stability,** and **Spirituality or Personal Growth**.

Next, use a pink highlighter to mark any areas needing attention and balance. These are the areas that may require more focus or improvement. Use a green highlighter to highlight areas that feel balanced and are contributing positively to your life. This exercise will help you visually see where you need to direct more energy to achieve a well-rounded and fulfilling life.

The 5-Year Letter: Write a letter to your future self, describing where you want to be in five years—emotionally, spiritually, financially, and personally. This exercise helps clarify your vision and inspire intentional steps forward. Use the outline on the following pages to help you get started.

Dear _____ (Read this 5 years from today's date _____),

Here's how I feel today, and how I hope to feel in five years:

ABOUT MY FINANCES

Right now, I feel: _____

In five years, I hope to feel: _____

ABOUT ROMANCE IN MY LIFE

Right now, I feel: _____

In five years, I hope to feel: _____

ABOUT BEING CREATIVE

Right now, I feel: _____

In five years, I hope to feel: _____

ABOUT HOW OFTEN I LAUGH

Right now, I feel: _____

CREATING A NEW ROADMAP

In five years, I hope to feel: _____

_____

ABOUT HOW MUCH JOY EXISTS FOR ME

Right now, I feel: _____

_____

In five years, I hope to feel: _____

_____

ABOUT HOW PEACEFUL I FEEL

Right now, I feel: _____

_____

In five years, I hope to feel: _____

_____

ABOUT MY PHYSICAL HEALTH & WELLBEING

Right now, I feel: _____

_____

In five years, I hope to feel: _____

_____

ABOUT THE QUALITY OF MY RELATIONSHIPS

Right now, I feel: _____

_____

In five years, I hope to feel: _____

_____

WHERE I'M FOCUSING MOST OF MY TIME AND ENERGY

Right now, I feel: _____

_____

In five years, I hope to feel: _____

_____

ABOUT HOW MUCH I LOVE MYSELF TODAY

Right now, I feel: _____

_____

In five years, I hope to feel: _____

_____

Keep this book, and set a reminder on your calendar to revisit it in five years. It'll be a powerful (and likely surprising) way to see how far you've come and how much you've evolved.

These practical exercises provide a structured way to clarify your vision, align your actions, and create a roadmap for meaningful growth and fulfillment.

How did it feel to write out the 5-Year Letter?

_____

_____

Would you recommend that exercise to others? _____

CHARTING A NEW COURSE

The Career Pivot: A mid-level manager left a stagnant job to pursue her passion for sustainable design. By creating a roadmap, she identified opportunities, built new skills, and launched a successful eco-friendly business.

The Holistic Transformation: A man facing ongoing health challenges transformed his life by setting small, consistent goals. Over time, he improved his physical, emotional, and mental well-being.

The Family Reconnection: A busy executive prioritized rebuilding relationships with his family. By scheduling regular quality time and open communication, he transformed his home life and rediscovered joy.

The Man Who Wanted More: A friend once asked how much money I wanted to make, and I replied, "*More.*" He pointed out that without a clear target, I'd always be in a state of wanting. Following his advice, I wrote down specific income and savings goals, then created a vision statement and hung it in my living room as a daily reminder. Defining my financial aspirations gave me a tangible roadmap, and as a result, I've far surpassed those goals.

Do you believe that charting a new course can create meaningful change in your life, whether in your career, health, relationships, or finances? _____

If so, write about a specific area in your life where you're ready to make a change. Are you willing to take the actionable steps outlined in this book and create your new path?

_____

_____

_____

Are you willing to take the actionable steps outlined in this book and create your new path? _____

THE PERCEPTUAL SHIFT

THE POWER OF ACTION

Creating a roadmap is only the beginning. The real transformation happens when you use your roadmap as a device to take consistent action toward your goals. Remember: *clarity without action is just potential*. It's the steps you take every day, no matter how small, that turn dreams into reality.

Progress Over Perfection: Focus on making steady progress rather than achieving perfection. Each small step builds momentum and brings you closer to your goals.

Celebrate Milestones: Acknowledge and reward your achievements along the way. Use your journal to record these moments, reflecting on how far you've come and inspiring yourself to keep moving forward.

Stay Committed: Keep your vision clear and steadfast. When the path becomes difficult, embrace failures as stepping stones and obstacles as hidden opportunities propelling you closer to realizing your dreams.

Reflect and Refine: Periodically review your roadmap to ensure it aligns with your evolving aspirations. Make time at regular intervals to adjust your strategies, celebrate progress, and refocus on what truly matters.

Formulating a new roadmap is a bold act of self-discovery and empowerment. It's a commitment to living intentionally, guided by your values and dreams. As you design your future, remember that the journey is just as important as the destination. Embrace the process, stay open to growth, and trust in your ability to create a life that reflects your highest potential.

Are you willing to create a roadmap and then act upon it? _____

If so, write down which of these you did, or are planning to do (The Vision Board, The "Perfect Day" Exercise, The Wheel of Life, or The 5-Year Letter).

_____

_____

Living in the Perceptual Shift

CULTIVATING A HABIT OF LOVE

There was an old man nearing the end of his life. It could be days at most, or perhaps just minutes, before whatever universal force had defined who he truly was would soon untangle itself from his body and return to the great mystery from which it came.

And he was okay with that.

As he lay there, quiet and calm, he reflected on the life he had lived. As a child, time moved slowly, like honey dripping from a spoon —slow and sweet. Summers stretched endlessly. Days felt like weeks. But now, in his eighties, life seemed to have rushed past in a blink. A beautiful blur of moments— some remembered vividly, some faded into feeling.

He imagined his life as a great puzzle. Each piece an image, a lesson, a memory. Some pieces were warm and bright: children laughing in sun-drenched parks, lovers picnicking under trees, and family gatherings filled with candles and cake. Christmas mornings. The first breath of spring

But there were darker pieces too.

A child weeping alone in the dark. A married woman running into the arms of someone else. An injured teenager lying in a hospital bed. Pieces that, at the time, seemed like mistakes—like they couldn't possibly belong in the picture of the life he thought he was building.

And yet... they did. Every piece had its place.

Even the ones that didn't seem to fit—those strange, painful, misunderstood moments—clicked perfectly into the full image. Scattered throughout the puzzle were quieter pieces imprinted with hearts and peace signs, of him standing in silent meditation, or opening his arms wide to the sky.

Looking back, he saw how often he had thought, "*This isn't how it's supposed to go.*" He resisted. He doubted. But now, with the whole picture visible, he saw how *every single moment* had led to something else—something beautiful, something necessary. Every joy, every loss, every wrong turn and right one, had carved a path toward understanding.

Urging him—

To dance more often.
To sing loudly, even off key.
To play like a child, often and without guilt.
To make time for mountains and oceans and trees.
To love with everything he had.
To share what he had without holding back.
To give time instead of excuses.
To laugh until he cried, and to cry without shame.
To never open the door when fear knocked.
And to smile—at strangers, at the sky, at himself.

He had done these things. Not all at once, and not always easily. But slowly, over the course of almost a century of experiences, he had lived his way into the life he was meant to love—a life of joy and sorrow, of stumbles and triumphs, of bold leaps and quiet grace. Through it all, he had loved with his whole heart. And he had wept deeply. That was the truth of it.

It was a good life.

And as he looked at the puzzle now, every piece in place, he felt something close to awe. He was proud—not because the puzzle was perfect, but because he had found the pieces that mattered most. The pieces that taught him how to truly, honestly, love his life. And that, he realized, was the secret to a life well-lived—not perfection, but presence. And in doing so, he had helped others learn how to love theirs.

LIVING IN THE PERCEPTUAL SHIFT

What he realized in those final moments is something many of us only glimpse in retrospect: every piece matters—but it's the ones that connect you back to love, gratitude, and peace that not only hold the puzzle together, but make the whole picture truly worthwhile.

Adopting a *Perceptual Shift* is the first step in transformation, but the real work lies in living it. Just as a puzzle isn't complete until every piece is placed, your personal transformation becomes whole through integration.

By consistently practicing daily rituals—your *"Daily Deal"*—a series of rituals like journaling, mindfulness, affirmations, movement, and visualization—you'll begin locking those pieces into place. These daily practices are your frame, your foundation. Grounded in self-love, they bring shape and order to the vision you've been forming.

Over time, these habits will help you cultivate a life of authenticity, joy, and abundance. They serve as anchors, keeping you grounded and empowering you to face challenges with the knowledge that everything will not only be okay, but it will actually be wonderful because you'll make it so.

Have you started putting any of these puzzle pieces—these habits and shifts—into your "Daily Deal"? _____

If yes, list the rituals you're practicing, how often you're doing them, and any changes you've noticed in your perception of life.

_____
_____
_____
_____
_____
_____

THE IMPORTANCE OF CONSISTENCY

Change doesn't happen overnight. Growth takes time—and the key is showing up. This isn't about perfection or always hitting your goals. It's about making the effort and realigning whenever you veer off course. Here's why staying consistent matters:

Rewire Your Brain: Repetition strengthens the neural pathways that support your new perspective, helping it become your natural default.

Build Momentum: Small, consistent actions compound over time, creating a ripple effect of meaningful transformation.

Strengthen Trust: Showing up for yourself builds internal trust—and the positive outcomes reinforce your commitment to *Living in the Shift*.

Think of consistency as the bridge between intention and transformation. It reinforces new perspectives, builds momentum, and nurtures faith in your ability to achieve your dreams. Cross that bridge, and you'll find yourself standing on the shore of possibility—bathed in the warmth of newfound clarity, joy, and abundance.

Have you noticed how inconsistency in your efforts leads to inconsistent results in your life? _____

*If so, write about a goal, aspiration, dream, or change you once pursued but didn't achieve due to inconsistency. How might **staying committed** have led to a different outcome?*

_____

_____

_____

_____

_____

PRACTICAL STRATEGIES FOR LIVING IN THE SHIFT

Living in the Shift means more than simply adopting a new perspective—it's about integrating that perspective into your daily life in meaningful, sustainable ways. These practical strategies will help you stay aligned with your *Perceptual Shift*, reinforcing gratitude, abundance, and resilience. By turning small, intentional actions into habits, you lay the groundwork for lasting transformation.

Start Each Day with Intention: Begin your day by setting an intention that aligns with your *Perceptual Shift*. For example, *"Today, I will approach challenges with curiosity and resilience."*

To help make this shift more tangible and deeply rooted in your daily life, here are some powerful practices embraced by *Perceptual Shifters*:

- *The "Thank You" Kiss:* Each morning, before even opening your eyes, reach your fingers to your lips, kiss them, and send the kiss upward. This simple gesture of gratitude creates a moment of intimacy with life—a quiet acknowledgment of the "divine romance" of existence.

  You've made it through the night, you're alive, and you have the opportunity—one that many do not—to embrace the beauty, challenges, and possibilities that lie ahead.

- *The Wiggle:* Start your day by gently moving your fingers and toes as soon as you wake up. Recognize and be grateful for the ability to move your body, a gift not everyone enjoys. This small moment of awareness connects you with your body and serves as a reminder of the blessings you might otherwise overlook.

- *Stretch:* Before hopping out of bed, take a few moments to stretch. Whether it's a deep, satisfying reach or a few gentle yoga movements, this practice helps you wake up your body with intention—rather than forcing it into action.

- *Meditate:* Set aside even just a few minutes for meditation. Research shows that as little as eight minutes of meditation can reduce stress, center your mind, and make up for as much as an hour of lost sleep. Whether it's focusing on your breath, a mantra, or a guided practice, this small act can make a big impact.

- *Affirmations:* Start your day with positive affirmations to counter self-doubt and reframe your mindset. For example, if you're struggling with finances, relationships, or joy, try saying, "I open myself up to the abundance of finance, romance, and happiness." Affirmations help shift your thoughts from "I can't" or "I'll never" to "I am" and "I will."

- *Mirror Work:* Stand in front of a mirror, look deeply into your own eyes, and say, "I love you. I love you so much!" To amplify this exercise, keep a photo of your younger self on the bathroom counter, kiss it, and express love to the child within you. Promise that child you'll make it a point to have some fun today. This can be incredibly healing, especially for those who may not have felt fully loved during childhood.

- *ILML (I Love My Life):* Shout out, *"I love my life!"* This joyful declaration reinforces gratitude and embodies the thought, word, and deed of love. By aligning your mindset, speech, and actions with love, you create a ripple effect of positivity that can inspire and uplift others who hear your enthusiasm.

- *Inspirational Reading:* Start your day by reading and reflecting on passages from inspirational books or daily readers. Highlight sections that resonate with you and revisit them often. This practice can shift your focus toward love, gratitude, and positivity, setting the tone for the rest of the day.

By the way, the word "inspiration" comes from the Latin inspirare, meaning "to breathe into," and refers to the act of breathing life or spirit into something. So by reading from inspirational books each morning, you're essentially breathing life, energy, and positivity into your mind, body and spirit, setting the tone for creativity, growth, and purpose.

These simple yet profound morning practices create a *"**Daily Deal**"* that anchors your day in gratitude and abundance, transforming your *Perceptual Shift* from a concept into a lived reality. Incorporating even a few of these habits into your morning routine can elevate your joy, peace, and fulfillment, making the rest of your day more intentional, abundant, and aligned with your highest self.

Surround Yourself with Support: Surrounding yourself with people who uplift, encourage, and embody the mindset you're cultivating is one of the most powerful ways to stay aligned with positivity and abundance.

Fellowship with like-minded individuals offers a sense of community, accountability, and shared energy that fuels your growth. Here are some advantages of fellowship:

- *Shared Energy:* Being around someone with positive energy can elevate your own mood and motivation. Their enthusiasm is contagious and strengthens your commitment to growth.

- *Accountability:* Having a like-minded friend can help you stay on track by holding you accountable to your goals and intentions.

- *Encouragement:* During challenging times, fellowship provides a safety net of encouragement and empathy, reminding you that you're not alone.

- *Diverse Perspectives:* Engaging with others allows you to gain new insights and ideas, broadening your understanding of abundance and positivity.

- *Celebrating Wins:* Sharing your successes, no matter how small, with someone who truly understands your journey makes your progress even more meaningful.

- *Collaborative Growth:* Working through challenges or new ideas with others creates a dynamic environment for mutual learning and self-discovery.

Discover and nurture fellowship by seeking out like-minded communities, participating in positive activities, and building meaningful connections with those who share your values and aspirations. Here are some ways to find and cultivate fellowship:

- *Join Positive Communities:* Seek out local groups or online communities that focus on personal growth, positivity, or abundance. Look for book clubs, meditation groups, nature walking meetups, or workshops aligned with your goals.

- *Engage in Activities That Attract Like-Minded People:* Join yoga classes, attend seminars, participate in volunteer work, or enjoy music concerts. Surrounding yourself with individuals who value positivity and creativity increases the likelihood of building meaningful connections.

- *Leverage Social Media and Online Platforms:* Networks like Facebook, Meetup, or even LinkedIn often host groups centered around personal growth and abundance practices. Engage in discussions and virtual meetups to expand your circle.

- *Host Your Own Circle:* Invite friends or acquaintances who share your vision to meet regularly and explore the ideas and exercises in this book. Use your time together to encourage, support, and hold each other accountable.

- *Mentorship and Guidance:* Seek out mentors or coaches who embody the mindset you're striving for. Learning from their experiences and guidance can significantly accelerate your journey.

- *Stay Open:* Sometimes support comes from unexpected places. Stay open to forming connections with colleagues, neighbors, or others who demonstrate a positive and growth-oriented mindset.

Fellowship involves actively participating in discussions, setting goals, celebrating achievements, and sharing resources with others committed to positivity and growth. These gatherings foster connection, encouragement, and momentum for both personal and collective transformation.

Here are some meaningful group activities.

- *Group Discussions:* Share reflections and insights from the exercises in this book. Discuss challenges, breakthroughs, and strategies for growth.
- *Collaborative Goal-Setting:* Set shared goals with your group and celebrate milestones together.
- *Accountability Partners:* Pair up with someone who can check in with you regularly, offering support and encouragement as you progress.
- *Host Themed Meetings:* Dedicate specific gatherings to topics like gratitude practices, meditation techniques, or affirmation creation.
- *Flash Card Discussions:* Write key ideas from this book—like journaling, meditation, or relationship shifts—on flashcards. Group members draw a card and share thoughts, experiences, and strategies.
- *Encourage Ongoing Learning:* Share books, articles, podcasts, or other resources that inspire and educate, keeping the energy of loving growth alive within the group.

By seeking fellowship and engaging with others who are on similar paths, you amplify your own journey. Together, you can spark a wave of positivity and abundance that uplifts not only your lives but also the lives of those around you.

Celebrate Progress: Acknowledge and celebrate the moments when you successfully embrace your new perspective, as this reinforces positive behavior and motivates you to keep moving forward. Use your journal to track these milestones. Reflect on your growth and note the specific actions or mindsets that led to your success. Journaling allows you to document your journey, providing a powerful reminder of how far you've come and inspiring you to continue embracing positivity and abundance.

As you commit to these practices, remember that every effort, no matter how small, contributes to your growth. Whether it's starting the day with a mindful intention, engaging in fellowship, or celebrating progress, each step strengthens your journey. By embracing these strategies with an open heart and a willing spirit, you're not just *Living the Shift*—you're embodying it, inspiring others along the way, and creating a life filled with joy, connection, and purpose.

Do you see how starting your day with a "*Daily Deal***" focused on gratitude, self-care, and intention can positively impact your relationships and interactions with others? _____**

If so, write about how surrounding yourself with people who embrace an abundance mindset and live in an attitude of gratitude could inspire you and transform your life. How might being part of a supportive, uplifting community influence your daily experience and personal growth?

_____
_____
_____
_____
_____
_____
_____
_____
_____
_____
_____
_____
_____

OVERCOMING LIFE'S CHALLENGES

Living in the Shift isn't always easy—but a willingness to grow makes all the difference. Old patterns and external pressures may try to pull you back into familiar ways of thinking. Here's how to overcome those common challenges:

Recognize Triggers: Pay attention to the situations, people, or habits that tempt you to slip back into outdated perceptions. When these arise, pause, apply your *Perceptual Shifting* tools, and if needed, detach with love.

Practice Self-Compassion: Be kind to yourself when you falter, recognizing that *growth is a process, not a destination*. Encourage yourself as you would a close friend, making the journey more supportive and fun.

Revisit Your Why: Remember why you chose to embrace *Perceptual Shifting*—whether to overcome challenges, love life more, create abundance, or all of the above. Stay focused on your transformation, and *no matter what*, don't give up before the miracle happens.

Seek Accountability: Share your goals with a trusted friend, coach, or mentor who can offer support and encouragement. Check in regularly with someone you trust—whether it's a friend, coach, or mentor—who can offer encouragement and accountability, especially when old habits start to creep back in.

Every challenge you overcome deepens your growth and brings you closer to lasting peace and fulfillment. *Keep going!*

Do you recognize areas in your life where old patterns still try to pull you back? _____

If so, write down one specific area you're ready to overcome, and how doing so could improve your life.

_____

_____

ALIGNING YOURSELF WITH YOUR SHIFT

Living in the Shift means bringing your life into harmony with your new perspective. This alignment fosters authenticity and empowers you to fully embody your transformation. Here's how to begin aligning the most important areas of your life with your new awareness and values, so that your outer world reflects the inner shift you're making.

Career: Consider whether your work aligns with your values and aspirations. If it doesn't, explore ways to adjust your path so your career supports both your fulfillment and your evolving perspective.

Relationships: Foster connections that uplift and inspire you. Communicate openly about your shift, and invite others into conversations that encourage mutual growth.

Health: Make your physical and mental well-being a foundational priority. Adopt habits that sustain your energy and resilience. Even a short nap can refresh your mind and body, keeping you aligned with your transformation.

Environment: Design your space to reflect your new mindset. A clean, organized, and inspiring environment fosters clarity, focus, and motivation, reinforcing your shift.

Aligning your life choices with the shift you're making creates harmony, reinforcing your transformation in every area—from career and relationships to health and environment.

Do you see how aligning your choices with love, gratitude, and growth can lead to greater happiness? _____

If so, write down one area of your life that feels out of alignment with your intended perspective shift.

_____

_____

THE RIPPLE EFFECT OF LIVING IN THE SHIFT

Your *Perceptual Shift* doesn't just transform your life; it also influences those around you. By embodying your new perspective, you:

Inspire Others: Few things are as influential as leading by example. When you embody *Perceptual Shifting*—through actions, attitude, and approach—you motivate others to reflect and consider new perspectives.

Demonstrating growth and authenticity inspires those around you, encouraging them to begin their own transformative journeys.

Foster Positive Change: Here are some areas of your life that can be positively impacted by shifting into a mindset of gratitude and abundance.

- *In Families:* A parent who models patience and gratitude inspires their children to approach challenges with a positive mindset, fostering a cycle of emotional resilience across generations.

- *In the Workplace:* A team member who shifts from criticism to collaboration encourages a more supportive and innovative work environment, often leading colleagues to adopt similar attitudes.

- *In Friendships:* A person who practices active listening and empathy deepens their connections, inspiring their friends to engage more openly and authentically with others.

- *In Communities:* Someone who embraces an abundance mindset and contributes to local causes can inspire neighbors to do the same, creating a collective uplift in well-being and connection.

- *In Social Circles:* Consistently expressing gratitude and kindness invites those around you to reflect on their own behaviors, creating a ripple of positivity and mutual support.

These shifts may begin subtly, but their impact can be profound, transforming your immediate circle and influencing the broader world. As more people utilize the art of *Perceptual Shifting* in their lives, the collective consciousness evolves, fostering greater compassion and connection.

Perceptual Shifts don't just influence those around us—they create profound changes within ourselves. When we shift our mindset from illness to health, focusing on healing rather than pain, our bodies respond. Science supports the reality that a positive, healing-focused mindset can accelerate recovery, reduce stress, and strengthen the immune system. Just as pain can spread through the body, healing in one area has the power to uplift and restore the whole. This internal transformation is the foundation for the external changes we bring to the world.

By fully engaging with the practices in this book, you not only transform your life but also inspire and uplift others, contributing to a more positive and harmonious world. And let's be honest—*it's also great karma*!

And remember—this is important because I've seen it happen too often: when this work brings you the amazing life you've always wanted, don't stop doing what got you there. Continual *Perceptual Shifting* is what keeps you growing, evolving, and sustaining the happiness you deserve.

Do you see how fully embodying your Perceptual Shift can both transform your life while inspiring those around you? _____

If so, think of one person you would love to inspire to shift their perspective toward greater abundance. Who would that person be, and why do you want to support their transformation?

_____

_____

_____

_____

THE ROLE OF REFLECTION

Just like a business that fails to take inventory or track its assets and liabilities, a person who avoids reflection is likely to struggle. Without examining what's thriving and what needs attention, it's easy to drift off course and repeat patterns that no longer serve you.

In-the-Moment Check-In: This is one of the most important exercises of all, especially in moments of discomfort. When you feel overwhelmed, triggered, or unsure how to respond, pause and check in with yourself. Use your journal to process these moments by following these four steps:

1. *What happened*—the event, circumstances, people, or anything else involved. If you feel like blaming someone or something, this is the place to do it.

2. *How it affected you*—your pride, relationships, finances, personal security, or sense of self-worth. How did it feel?

3. *Your part* in the situation. If you don't see one, consider possibilities like not detaching quickly enough, having expectations, or making a choice that contributed to the outcome.

4. *What you'll do differently next time* in order to avoid repeating the same experience. We only have the power to change ourselves.

Once you've completed these steps, lightly cross out the first two—what happened and how it affected you—so the focus remains on your part and your opportunity to grow. This visual shift reinforces your power to grow from the experience rather than dwell on it.

Then, look for a chance to make amends, if possible. It shouldn't be something to dread—it's an opportunity to make things right. Contrary to what many believe, taking responsibility and making amends is often the quickest way to feel better, allowing you to release resentment and return to the business of loving life.

Daily Check-Ins: In the evening, reflect on the day's successes and the moments where you learned by turning obstacles into opportunities. This is also the perfect time to acknowledge personal growth and write down ways you handled challenges with more grace than you might have in the past. If you're more of a morning person, use that time to reflect on the previous day's experiences and set intentions for building on your progress.

Monthly Reviews: Once a month, set aside time to assess your progress and realign with your goals. Write about the shifts you've made, the milestones you've achieved, and any recurring challenges that might need extra attention. This is best done **in ink**, making your journey tangible and trackable. Adjust your strategies, refine your intentions, and set new, actionable goals that keep you moving forward with clarity and purpose.

Gratitude Journaling: Writing down the positive changes your *Perceptual Shift* has brought into your life reinforces your commitment to growth and helps you stay attuned to the abundance around you. If you ever struggle to come up with things to be grateful for, try listing parts of your body, your favorite foods, or elements of nature that bring you joy.

Consider sharing your gratitude list with others who are on this journey. I personally text mine to friends who appreciate receiving them—and they text me theirs. This exchange strengthens connections, fosters mutual encouragement, and spreads positivity in a way that uplifts everyone involved.

Gratitude is always available—it just takes a moment to notice what's already beautiful.

Seek Feedback: Invite input from trusted friends, mentors, or accountability partners to gain new perspectives on your journey. However, be mindful to seek feedback only from those who genuinely support your growth and understand your commitment to *Perceptual Shifting*.

Avoid sharing with individuals who might be dismissive, critical, or inclined to offer unsolicited advice that could undermine your progress.

Even if writing in a journal regularly feels uncomfortable or difficult, I encourage you to lean into the discomfort and try anyway. Over time, it will become easier, and your journal will start to feel like a trusted friend—one that offers valuable insights and honest feedback.

By actively reflecting on your experiences and refining your approach, you empower yourself to live in alignment with your vision. Journaling your thoughts, taking ownership of your actions, and celebrating progress—even the small wins—will keep you centered on your path to loving life and creating abundance. This is where the practice becomes real. This is how your shift becomes lasting

Are you willing to start journaling on a regular basis, even if it feels uncomfortable? ____

If so, create a basic journal entry by filling out the following prompts:

Today's Date: _____

The Time: _____

Where You're Sitting: _____

How You Feel: _____

One Accomplishment From Today: _____

One Thing You're Grateful For: _____

Write "I love my life!" (even if you don't): _____

How did it feel to do that?

_____

_____

When short on time, a quick check-in like the one above can boost your sense of accomplishment and support consistency in caring for yourself.

THE PERCEPTUAL SHIFT

INSPIRING STORIES OF TRANSFORMATION

From Overwhelm to Clarity

Samantha, a first-time mother of twins, felt overwhelmed by exhaustion and self-doubt. Sleepless nights and endless responsibilities left her questioning whether she could manage it all. Her once-loving home now felt chaotic, and her relationship with her husband had become strained.

One evening, she discovered **Perceptual Shifting**—the practice of reframing her experience and focusing on what was going right. She began seeing the messy house as proof of a home filled with love. She paused for deep breaths during stressful moments and wrote down small joys each night in gratitude.

She and her husband also started **Daily Check-Ins**, both individually and together—replacing complaints with expressions of appreciation. This strengthened their bond, shifting their dynamic from frustration to teamwork. Samantha prioritized self-care, adjusted her sleep expectations, and found joy in simple moments—warm coffee, baby giggles, and dancing in the kitchen .

Through small, intentional shifts, completely transformed her reality. "I may not control every situation," she says, "but I can choose how I see my life. And that has made all the difference."

Do you see how changing the way Samantha was thinking about her situation completely shifted her experience? _____

What's the one, most important tool that you would like to always use if a similar type of situation happens to you?

_____

_____

_____

Rebuilding After Loss

When a fire destroyed Daniel's restaurant and home, it felt like his entire life had gone up in flames. Overwhelmed and uncertain, he struggled with grief and hopelessness. But one night, staring at the ashes, he realized he had a choice: stay stuck in despair or rebuild—not just as it was, but better.

And so, Daniel reframed the loss as an opportunity for transformation. He envisioned a home built around family connection and a restaurant with improved systems and a menu that honored his community. By sharing his vision, he inspired his family and team to believe in a new beginning.

He sought grants, engaged his loyal clients on social media, and received overwhelming support. Volunteers and disaster relief programs assisted him in beginning the rebuilding process. His team enhanced the restaurant, while an architect volunteered to design a thoughtful new home.

Throughout the process, Daniel practiced gratitude, journaling small victories that reinforced his belief in a brighter future. When the new restaurant opened, it became a symbol of resilience. Customers returned, employees thrived, and his family embraced their new space, stronger than before.

Reflecting on his journey, Daniel said, *"The fire took everything—but it also gave me the chance to rebuild with intention. By shifting my perspective, I didn't just rebuild my life; I reimagined it into something even better."*

Would you agree that having more tools to shift your perspective in the face of tragedy leads to a better outcome? _____

Thinking about Daniel's experience, how do you think he was able to shift so well, considering all that had happened to him?

_____

_____

_____

Healing Through Forgiveness

Mike and Lisa had been close friends with Jack and Sarah for over 15 years. Their families were inseparable. So when Jack and Sarah fell on hard times, Mike and Lisa didn't hesitate to lend them $10,000—even though it strained their own finances. Then Jack and Sarah moved away—unexpectedly—and cut off all communication. Calls went unanswered. Resentment grew.

One day, Lisa learned about **Perceptual Shifting** and suggested reframing their loss. Instead of dwelling on betrayal, they chose to see the loan as a gift given in kindness. This shift eased their resentment, allowing them to focus on gratitude and move forward.

Years later, they received a letter from Jack with a $500 check and an apology. He explained that after moving, their daughter had tragically passed away, sending Sarah into deep depression. Now, with stability returning, he wanted to make amends.

Mike and Lisa, overwhelmed with emotion, let go of any lingering resentment. Lisa later reflected, *"If we hadn't shifted our perspective, we might still be bitter, unable to see beyond our pain. Forgiveness freed us, bringing peace, compassion—and reconnection."*

By changing their perspective, they not only found healing but also rekindled a lost friendship, proving that true forgiveness opens the door to reconciliation.

Is there someone you've had trouble forgiving? _____

If so, write their name(s) below and describe how you think you would feel if you were able to fully forgive them and release the hurt from the past.

_____

_____

_____

_____

ADAPTING TO THE ROAD AHEAD

Living in the Shift is an ongoing journey of growth, discovery, and alignment. It requires intention, effort, and flexibility—but the rewards are profound. By consistently integrating your new perspective into daily life, you build a strong foundation for lasting joy, abundance, and authenticity.

Remember, the journey of *Perceptual Shifting* isn't about perfection—it's about progress. Embrace each step with curiosity and gratitude. Trust that every effort moves you closer to the life you've been envisioning. Your commitment to *Living in the Shift* isn't just a gift to yourself. It's a contribution to a more compassionate and inspired world.

As mentioned earlier, setbacks and challenges are part of the path—not signs of failure. Growth is a cycle. Every moment offers a chance to pause, reflect, and realign with your vision. When doubts arise, return to your tools. Return to gratitude. Return to your deeper *why*. The more you embrace the shift, the more natural it becomes—until one day, you look back and realize you're living the life you once only dreamed of.

Do you see how the transformative experience of Perceptual Shifting can profoundly change the way you see life and how you act, ultimately creating a new, better version of yourself? _____

If so, write about one way in which you already feel yourself shifting. How has this change impacted your thoughts, emotions, actions or relationships?

_____

_____

_____

_____

_____

You've now stepped into the heart of the practice—Living in the Shift. This chapter marked a powerful turning point, where your insights and reflections begin taking root in your daily actions, your relationships, your rituals, and your mindset.

Here's what this chapter reinforced:

- Integration is key—daily rituals and consistency help solidify your transformation.
- Fellowship and community offer support, encouragement, and accountability.
- Flexibility is a superpower—adapting with grace keeps you aligned with your vision.
- Reflection deepens awareness and reinforces the shifts you're making.
- Your journey impacts others—living in the Shift creates a ripple effect that spreads love, compassion, and inspiration.
- Perceptual Shifting isn't a destination—it's a way of seeing, living, and being.

The more you practice shifting, the more natural it becomes—until one day, you realize that you no longer have to 'try' to love your life. You just do.

Do you feel like you're starting to live your life with more intention and alignment? _____

If so, write about one area of your life where this shift is becoming evident. How does it feel different now compared to before you began this journey?

_____

_____

_____

_____

_____

Envisioning Your Abundant Life
FINDING THE BURIED TREASURES

Abundance isn't solely about material wealth—though financial prosperity can be a wonderful part of it. True abundance is both a mindset and a way of living that embraces the richness of life in all its diverse forms. Whether it's the love of family and friends, the beauty of nature, the fulfillment of meaningful work, or the joy of personal growth, abundance surrounds us when we choose to recognize and appreciate it.

Understanding what abundance means to you is essential. Without a personal definition, it's easy to chase someone else's version of success—only to find it doesn't align with your heart's true desire. By taking the time to learn about, and reflect on what abundance looks and feels like in your life, you gain clarity on what truly matters.

Two friends, Brett and Cameron, graduated college together—both bright, ambitious, and full of possibility. Life took them in different directions, and for many years, they lost touch.

Brett climbed fast. With sharp instincts and relentless drive, he broke into the world of high-stakes business. Every year brought more—deals, recognition, status, money… and more beautiful women. His life became a blur of parties, luxury penthouses, award galas, and adrenaline-charged negotiations.

As his power grew, so did the demands. His phone rang late into the night. His schedule was stacked with meetings, flights, and mergers. He bought homes around the world, a fleet of cars, and even a jet with his initials etched on the side. On paper, Brett had it all—abundance beyond anything he'd imagined.

But his world was ruthless, and to survive in it, he became the same. He got married and divorced three times—he called it *"getting upgrades."* His children stopped calling. He smiled on magazine covers, gave interviews on financial news shows, and started showing up on talk shows as the face of modern success.

His name was known. His company, praised. His empire, solid. People even began talking about him running for President.

His college friend, Cameron, had taken a different path—one that rarely made headlines.

After graduation, Cameron joined a small real estate firm focused on sustainable housing and urban farming. They turned rooftops into gardens, vacant lots into orchards, and abandoned warehouses into vibrant greenhouses. They built affordable housing with integrated growing spaces—raised beds, shared plots, vertical gardens—and helped residents learn how to grow their own food. Volunteers came to teach, to harvest, to celebrate.

Cameron never made much money. Eventually, he and his wife moved into one of the communities they helped create. She became an urban farming consultant. They raised two children, never got divorced, and were known and loved by their neighbors. Every year, they held a harvest festival—music, laughter, potlucks, and hugs from families they had once helped get a fresh start.

One afternoon, in a quiet coffee shop during a rare unscheduled hour, Brett looked up—and there was Cameron.

"*Whoa, man, it's Cameron,*" Brett said, standing up with a grin, "*I saw you on TV. Congratulations. You've done it. You have everything you wanted!*"

"*Thanks Cameron,*" Brett replied with a warm smile. "*So what have you been up to?*"

"Oh, this and that," Cameron smiled. "*You remember the girl I was dating our last year of college? I married her.*"

"*No kidding!*"

"*Yeah. We have two kids—Annie and Jake. Annie just graduated with a degree in Entertainment Management. She's engaged—getting married next year. Jake went to med school. He's about to start his residency in Texas. He and his wife, Amy, gave me a beautiful granddaughter. I'm a grandpa now.*"

Brett blinked. "*Wow.*"

Cameron continued, "*I ended up working with a real estate development group that focuses on sustainable housing—urban gardens, community spaces, food security. We moved into one of the communities we helped create. My wife consults on urban farming. We've built something that matters. And we're surrounded by people who love us.*"

Brett stared into his coffee. For a long time, he didn't say a word.

"*You okay, man?*" Cameron asked.

Brett exhaled slowly. "*Yeah. Just thinking. I have three kids… but I barely know them. Three ex-wives who pretty much hate me. All the money in the world, but I wish I'd taken your path. You seem so… content in your life.*"

Cameron leaned forward gently. "*Brett… it's never too late to start over. You can still choose a different kind of abundance.*"

Brett looked up, eyes heavy. "*You really think so? I wouldn't even know how to start.*"

"*I do. Come over for dinner this week. Meet my family and let's talk.*"

They hugged before parting ways—one returning to an abundant garden waited to be harvested, the other returning to a very different kind of abundance.
In this chapter, we'll explore what it means to cultivate an abundance mindset, and practical ways to manifest and sustain a life filled with joy, purpose, and fulfillment.

Together, we'll reflect on the difference between having an *abundance of things*—money, property, prestige—and living an *abundant life* rooted in meaning, connection, and gratitude.

The two aren't mutually exclusive—you can have both. But without a clear understanding of what *your* version of abundance truly is, it's easy to chase what looks good on the outside and miss what feels good on the inside.

The exercises and reflections that follow are here to help you define abundance on your own terms and begin living it in real time.

Do you see the difference between an abundance of things—which may give you a life that looks successful—and an abundant life, which lets you to feel truly fulfilled, alive, and at peace? _____

Take a moment to define what abundance means to you—right now, in this season of your life.

_____

_____

_____

_____

_____

_____

_____

_____

_____

At the end of the chapter, we'll return to this same question to see if anything has shifted.

TYPES OF ABUNDANCE

Abundance is often misunderstood as merely accumulating wealth or material possessions, but it is so much more. True abundance is a mindset—a way of experiencing life that touches every aspect of our being. It's about recognizing and appreciating the richness already present while remaining open to receiving even more in ways that uplift and nourish us. Some forms of abundance include:

Abundance in Health: Experiencing vitality, strength, and wellness in your physical and mental well-being. Health abundance arises when we nurture our body, mind, and spirit through self-care, balance, and healthy habits. Recognize the wealth in your ability to move, breathe, and engage with the world.

Emotional Abundance: This expands in direct proportion to the energy we invest in cultivating joy, love, and gratitude as a consistent part of your daily experience. It's about finding contentment and peace within, regardless of external circumstances. Emotional abundance allows you to face challenges with resilience and an open heart.

Relational Abundance: Relationships grounded in trust, mutual respect, and support—whether with family, friends, colleagues, or romantic partners—are a vital part of life. It takes effort to create and nurture deep, meaningful connections with others, but it's so worthwhile.

Creative Abundance: We unlock our inner potential by pursuing our passions and expressing ourselves authentically. Whether through art, problem-solving, or innovation, creative abundance fuels personal growth and brings fulfillment by allowing you to share your unique gifts with the world.

Spiritual Abundance: Feeling connected to a higher purpose, the universe, or whatever resonates from a place of love. It's about recognizing the interconnectedness of life and finding peace and meaning in that connection, guiding you toward a more profound understanding of yourself and your place in the world.

Material Abundance: Having the physical and financial resources necessary to meet your needs, pursue your dreams, and share generously with others. Material abundance isn't about excess—it's about sufficiency, freedom, comfort, and the ability to uplift others while living a life aligned with your values.

By expanding your understanding of abundance to include these diverse forms, you open space for all of it to enter your life. This shift invites you to experience life more fully—through gratitude, connection, and the mindset of limitless possibility.

Do you see how abundance extends far beyond material wealth and touches every area of your life? _____

If so, choose one area—health, emotional, relational, creative, spiritual, or material—that you'd most like to expand. What small actions can you take this week to nurture more of it in your life?

_____

_____

_____

_____

_____

_____

_____

_____

_____

_____

_____

_____

THE MINDSET OF ABUNDANCE

Living abundantly begins with cultivating an abundance mindset. This means *shifting your focus away from scarcity*—what you lack—and toward gratitude for what you have, along with trust in what's possible. Abundance isn't just about material wealth; it's a perspective that invites more joy, love, and opportunity into your daily experience. Here are a few ways to begin cultivating an abundance mindset:

Trust in Limitless Abundance: The universe is vast, and opportunities are everywhere. When you shift from scarcity to trust, you begin noticing possibilities that once felt hidden. This mindset helps attract experiences, relationships, and success aligned with your highest aspirations.

Practice Daily Gratitude: Your mind is like a *magic magnifying glass*—whatever you focus on expands. By regularly acknowledging your blessings, even the small ones, you shift your perception toward abundance. Consider keeping a gratitude journal, listing at least three things you appreciate each day. Share your gratitude with others to spark a ripple effect of positivity.

Visualize Your Dreams: Each day, imagine your ideal life in vivid detail. Connect emotionally with the feeling of already having what you desire. To keep your focus clear, create and update a vision board that brings your dreams and goals to life through imagery and words.

Reframe Negative Thoughts: When challenges arise, pause and shift your perspective. Rather than thinking, *"I'll never succeed,"* try, *"Every step I take brings me closer to success."* Instead of assuming someone's behavior is meant to hurt you, consider that they may be struggling with their own battles. This mental shift empowers you to navigate life with resilience and self-compassion.

Embrace Generosity: Sharing your time, resources, and gifts creates a flow of abundance. The more you give, the more you grow—kindness multiplies, and abundance flows. Giving freely—whether through time, service, or gifts—builds a deeper sense of fulfillment and connection.

Let Go of Comparison: Comparing yourself to others often leads to frustration and self-doubt. You never see the full picture of someone else's life—what appears effortless may have taken years of struggle. Instead of feeling envious, celebrate their success as proof that abundance is possible for everyone. Wishing others well shifts your mindset from competition to inspiration, reinforcing your belief in life's unlimited opportunities.

Celebrate Every Win: Acknowledge and celebrate progress, no matter how small. Achievements—big or small—build momentum, reinforcing positive habits and strengthening your confidence in creating abundance.

Celebrate Others' Successes: Instead of feeling envious, take joy in the abundance others experience. This is good sportsmanship. It reinforces your belief in the universe's infinite possibilities. Expressing genuine happiness for others' success strengthens your own self-worth, reinforcing the belief that their achievements don't diminish your value but inspire mutual growth.

An abundance mindset goes beyond positive thinking—it's about embodying abundance through your actions, words, and responses to life. By practicing gratitude, visualizing your dreams, and shifting your thoughts toward possibility, you align yourself with the energy of prosperity.

The more you integrate these habits into your daily life, the more natural they become, shaping the way you experience the world. Abundance isn't something you wait for—it's something you step into, cultivate, and invite to flow *through* and *around* you.

Do you see how shifting from scarcity to abundance can open the door to more joy, opportunity, and fulfillment? _____

If so, write about one area of your life where you feel something is missing. What feeling do you hope to experience when that space is filled?

_____

_____

_____

MANIFESTING ABUNDANCE

Manifestation is the process of turning your desires into reality by aligning your thoughts, emotions, and actions. Here's how to begin manifesting abundance with intention and clarity:

Set Clear Intentions: Be clear and specific about your desires. In your affirmations, replace vague statements like *"I want to be successful"* concrete, meaningful goals that match your vision. Clarity directs your energy and helps turn intention into reality.

Align Your Actions: Manifestation is a dance between intention and action. Take consistent steps toward your goals—do the footwork, show up daily, and celebrate small wins along the way. Each action reinforces your commitment and momentum.

Embrace Positivity: Maintain a hopeful and optimistic outlook, even in the tough times. Challenges are stepping stones, not roadblocks—they push you to grow, build resilience, and develop the skills required to achieve your goals and reach your fullest potential. They also offer valuable lessons needed to reach your fullest potential.

Trust the Timing: We often want things to happen on our own schedule—whether it's love, career breakthroughs, or clarity during a tough time. But the universe follows its own rhythm, one that often serves a greater purpose we can't yet see.

What seems like a delay is often preparation—aligning the pieces for your highest good. When you surrender to divine timing, you release stress and find peace in the waiting. Trust that everything will happen when the time is right.

The word *divine* can carry religious meaning, but here, it's meant more broadly. It refers to the natural order, universal intelligence, or interconnected flow of life—a force beyond our immediate control that guides how things unfold. You don't need to be religious to embrace this concept;

it's simply a reminder that some things happen on a higher timeline, one that often serves us better than we imagined.

By aligning with life's natural flow, you create space for peace, clarity, and possibility—regardless of your spiritual or philosophical beliefs.

Manifesting abundance isn't just about attracting external success—it's about cultivating a mindset that helps you recognize the richness already present. With clear intentions, aligned action, and trust in timing, you move from longing to fulfillment.

The more you embrace life with gratitude and confidence, the more naturally abundance flows your way. Manifestation isn't just about getting—it's about becoming the version of yourself who effortlessly attracts what they desire. Whether you're calling in deeper relationships, greater financial freedom, or a more meaningful life, everything you seek is already within reach. This work simply opens you to receive it.

Do you see how manifestation goes beyond wishful thinking—and combines clarity, action, and trust? _____

If so, write down one specific desire you'd like to manifest.

_____

_____

_____

_____

_____

Would you be willing to add it to your morning abundance affirmations (e.g., "I open myself up to abundance. Abundance of...") to reinforce your intention daily? _____

ABUNDANCE IN RELATIONSHIPS

Relationships are a vital part of an abundant life. True relational abundance doesn't come from expecting others to meet our needs—it comes from bringing trust, respect, love, and support into the relationship ourselves. And while we may wish others would do the same, our willingness to show up with these qualities often—though not always—inspires them to rise with us, creating deeper mutual connection. Here are some ways to cultivate abundance in your connections:

Practice Active Listening: Give people your full attention and seek to understand their perspective. This is especially important when someone is upset with you—especially if you've tended to respond with defensiveness in the past.

When they finish speaking—or after a brief pause—try restating what you heard to show you're listening and genuinely trying to understand their feelings. Listen not just with your ears, but with your heart—for the feelings behind the words. That's the part that matters most and builds connection.

Often, even if it seems like they're asking you to change, what they truly want is to feel heard, acknowledged, and understood. Whether or not you decide to change, focus on listening with your heart, not just your head.

Express Gratitude: Regularly thank those who enrich your life. Expressing appreciation builds trust, deepens intimacy, and strengthens the connection through mutual respect.

You may notice that gratitude is a recurring theme throughout this book—and it won't be the last time it's mentioned. That's because cultivating an *Attitude of Gratitude* is one of the fundamental principles underlying *Perceptual Shifting*.

Gratitude has the power to transform how you view your experiences, relationships, and challenges, helping you focus on abundance rather than lack. By making gratitude a daily practice, you align yourself with positivity, open the door to greater joy, and pave the way for deeper personal growth.

Set Healthy Boundaries: For many, the idea of setting boundaries can feel daunting, especially if it's unfamiliar territory or past attempts have been met with resistance. The truth is, there are key considerations to keep in mind when establishing boundaries and following through with consequences, particularly if this behavior is new in an established relationship. Done thoughtfully, however, boundaries are a powerful tool in creating healthier, more abundant connections and fostering personal growth.

Here are some key points to consider:

Expect Resistance: Initially setting boundaries in a relationship where they haven't existed before is often met with resistance. This is natural, as others may need time to adjust to the new dynamic. Anticipate pushback, but remain calm and consistent—it's part of the process.

Choose Your Battles Wisely: Not every issue requires a boundary. Avoid overusing them or creating drama by trying to control every aspect of a relationship. Start with one or two areas that are most important to you, and once you've successfully set and enforced those, you can evaluate whether additional boundaries are needed.

Stay Firm: Once you've communicated a boundary and its consequence, follow through without wavering. It often takes just a few consistent actions for someone to understand you're serious. For example, if you say, *"I'm hanging up now,"* then don't hesitate—follow through immediately. Failing to act on your words teaches others that your boundaries can be ignored.

Be Prepared for Potential Endings: It's important to know that some relationships may not survive new boundaries. If someone refuses to honor certain boundaries—like continuing verbal abuse despite clear limits—choosing to walk away may be the healthiest path for your well-being.

Accepting the possibility of such outcomes and preparing for them reinforces your commitment to your values and emotional health. It empowers you to build relationships rooted in mutual respect and aligned with your needs. You, like everyone else, deserve healthy, loving relationships that support your well-being and growth.

Setting boundaries is a powerful act of *Perceptual Shifting*—transforming communication from a battle to win into a tool for empowerment, connection, and clarity. By clearly defining and upholding limits, you foster relationships rooted in trust, respect, and understanding, while detaching from those who choose not to honor them. This practice prioritizes your well-being, aligns your connections with your values, and creates space for growth, abundance, and positivity.

Just as a healthy garden requires the removal of weeds, staying away from toxicity—whether it's drama, negativity, or toxic people—is essential to cultivating happiness and peace. Loving others should never come at the expense of loving yourself. Surrounding yourself with people who embody positivity creates a supportive, thriving environment. And if a relationship ends, trust that new, healthier ones will take its place—aligned with your growth, your joy, and your abundance.

Be Generous: Give freely. Generosity expands and reflects, often returning to you in beautiful, unexpected ways. One of the most meaningful ways to share is by opening up about your journey into shifting perspectives, taking responsibility for your happiness, and manifesting abundance. Here are some ideas to inspire and guide you:

- *Start a Conversation:* Share your experiences casually with friends, family, or colleagues. Talk about the habits you've adopted and the positive changes you've noticed. Your enthusiasm may inspire them to explore their own paths to growth.

- *Use Social Media:* Write posts or create videos sharing your story, favorite practices, and insights. Highlight the new habits you've embraced—like gratitude journaling, daily affirmations, or meditative reflection—and the results they've brought into your life.

- *Invite Others to Join You:* Host a small gathering or discussion group where you can share concepts from your journey and explore them together. Consider using this book or other resources to guide the conversation and encourage shared growth.

- *Create a Gratitude Circle:* Form a group with like-minded friends where you regularly exchange gratitude lists. This practice helps everyone stay focused on the positive and deepens connections through mutual support.

- *Lead by Example:* Sometimes the best way to share is simply by embodying the changes. When others see you living with joy, peace, and abundance, they'll naturally want to know more about how you've achieved it.

- *Write About It:* Whether it's a blog, an article, or a personal email to someone close, putting your journey into words can clarify your own growth while inspiring others.

- *Offer Support:* Reach out to someone who seems stuck or struggling and share what has worked for you. Be careful not to impose your ideas, but offer your story as a source of encouragement and hope.

- *Celebrate Successes Together:* Share your milestones and celebrate them with those who support you. Acknowledging your wins can inspire others to notice and celebrate their own progress. Acknowledging theirs can strengthen relationships, creating an uplifting environment where everyone feels appreciated and empowered to grow.

- *Recommend Resources:* Share books, podcasts, videos, or other tools that have helped you along the way. Offering these resources shows that you're invested in helping others grow too.

- *Be Vulnerable:* Don't just share your wins—open up about the struggles you've faced and what helped you through them. Authenticity, paired with insight, can powerfully inspire and connect.

Sharing your journey isn't just about helping others; it deepens your own commitment to your shift. Every time you talk about your progress, gratitude and the wonderful results you're experiencing, you reinforce your growth and inspire a ripple effect of positivity in the world around you.

Be True to Yourself: Give freely, as mentioned above, knowing that generosity often leads to receiving, but never at the expense of self-love or self-care. Giving to others is a beautiful and rewarding act, but it should come from a place of abundance within yourself—not from sacrifice or obligation.

Remember, you cannot pour from an empty cup. Saying no when you don't want to do something isn't selfish; it's an act of self-respect that ensures you're able to give authentically and sustainably. Prioritizing your own well-being allows you to show up for others with a full heart, making your generosity even more meaningful.

Abundant relationships thrive on trust, respect, gratitude, and generosity. By listening actively, expressing appreciation, and setting healthy boundaries, you create deeper connections. True abundance comes from showing up as your best self, leading with love, and fostering relationships that uplift and inspire.

Do you see how gratitude, boundaries, and generosity work together to create deeper, more meaningful relationships? _____

If so, write which relationships in your life could benefit most from a shift.

_____

_____

_____

What's one way you can show up differently—more grounded in love, clarity, or kindness?

_____

_____

OVERCOMING SCARCITY THINKING

Scarcity thinking is a mindset rooted in fear and the belief that there's not enough—whether it's money, time, love, or opportunity. It often leads to feelings of inadequacy, comparison, and anxiety, making it difficult to recognize or receive abundance when it actually *is* present.

This mindset can show up in many ways—from hesitating to pursue a dream job out of fear, to feeling envious of someone else's success because it seems like there's less available for you. The good news is that scarcity thinking is a habit, and like any habit, it can be changed with intention and effort. Here's how to shift away from this limiting perspective:

Identify Limiting Beliefs: Write down recurring thoughts that reflect scarcity, such as: *"I'm not good enough,"* or *"Opportunities never come my way."*

_____

_____

Challenge that belief: Ask yourself, *"Is this really true?"* (Hint: The answer is no.) Reframe it into something empowering—like *"My potential is limitless"* or *"Opportunities are just around the corner."*

_____

_____

Focus on Opportunities: Train your mind to seek out possibilities and solutions rather than obstacles. Even in difficult situations, look for the lessons or opportunities for growth. Finding gratitude amidst challenges can transform problems into stepping stones toward abundance.

Surround Yourself with Positivity: Surround yourself with people, media, and environments that uplift and inspire abundance. Be mindful of negative influences that feed scarcity thinking, and limit your exposure to them. Set boundaries around what you no longer wish to consume or engage with—and honor those boundaries by gracefully detaching when needed.

Celebrate What You Have: Regularly acknowledge and celebrate the abundance already present in your life. Keep a daily gratitude list to remind yourself of the richness in your relationships, achievements, and even simple joys. Sharing your lists with others can inspire them to do the same.

When you shift your focus from fear and lack to gratitude and possibility, you create space for abundance to flow into your life. This perspective shift not only changes how you see the world—it helps you attract and embrace more opportunities for joy, growth, and fulfillment.

Do you recognize any areas in your life where scarcity thinking has held you back? _____

If so, write down one belief rooted in scarcity. Then reframe it into a positive, empowering statement that aligns with abundance. For example: "I never have enough time" → "I have the power to create time for what truly matters."

_____
_____
_____
_____
_____
_____
_____
_____
_____

THE PERCEPTUAL SHIFT

PRACTICAL EXERCISES FOR LIVING ABUNDANTLY

Living abundantly isn't just a mindset—it's a practice. By intentionally incorporating small rituals and habits into your daily life, you begin reinforcing a deeper sense of abundance, gratitude, and possibility.

These practices will help you focus on the richness already present in your life, cultivate a spirit of generosity, and embrace the boundless opportunities around you. Whether through journaling, visualization, or small acts of giving, these exercises empower you to align your thoughts, emotions, and actions with an abundant life.

The Abundance Journal: Each day, jot down moments where you felt abundant—big or small—and what sparked them. This trains your mind to notice abundance in all its forms: wealth, connection, joy, creativity, even peaceful moments. Over time, this practice shifts your focus from scarcity to gratitude. Revisit past entries often to remind yourself of how much richness already surrounds you.

The Abundance Chart: Create a visual map of all the areas in your life where you currently experience abundance. Use words, photos, magazine clippings, or your own drawings. Include relationships, accomplishments, personal strengths, resources, and opportunities. Add to your chart regularly as your awareness and experience of abundance grow.

The Generosity Challenge: Commit to a daily act of generosity—whether it's a kind word, a heartfelt compliment, a small favor, or a gesture of support. True abundance flows when you give freely from the heart. This practice reinforces the belief that there's always enough to share, and deepens your sense of connection, fulfillment, and joy.

Abundance Meditation: Set a timer for 10 minutes, close your eyes, and vividly imagine how it would feel to live in the abundance you desire. Focus on the emotions—joy, peace, love, fulfillment—and allow yourself to fully feel them. As you visualize, affirm your trust in the limitless abundance of the universe and your ability to welcome it into your life.

Abundance Affirmation Ritual: Stand outside or by a window. Take a deep breath, and slowly raise your arms toward the sky, opening them as if they were a chalice. Say the following aloud

"I open myself up to abundance—abundance of love, creativity, financial prosperity, joy, laughter, romance, and purpose. I release all resistance and allow abundance to flow freely into my life. I welcome it with gratitude."

Pause. Stay in this moment. Feel the energy of possibility flowing into you. Trust that by simply *allowing*, you are opening the channel for abundance to flow—naturally and effortlessly.

Abundance isn't something you chase—it's something you recognize, nurture, and embody. By consistently practicing these exercises, you'll reinforce the belief that abundance is already present, and even more is on its way. The more you engage with these practices, the more natural they become—and the more effortlessly abundance will begin to appear in your reality. Trust in the process, stay open to possibility, and watch as your world expands in ways you never imagined.

Do you see how actively engaging in abundance exercises can shift your mindset and attract more fulfillment into your life? _____

If so, and you've already completed one of the exercises in this section, take a moment to reflect. What did you experience? How did it feel? Write down any insights or emotional shifts that came up during the process. If you haven't done one yet, choose one now and give it a try.?

_____

_____

_____

_____

STORIES OF ABUNDANT LIVING

Abundance shows up in countless ways—and it often begins with a simple shift in perspective. The stories that follow illustrate how adopting an abundance mindset can transform lives, opening the door to creativity, connection, and resilience. Let them remind you that abundance is already present in your life—and that you have the power to welcome even more.

The Artist's Breakthrough: A struggling artist once focused solely on financial lack. But when she began celebrating her creativity and sharing her work freely, she attracted opportunities she never expected—and built a thriving career rooted in passion and purpose.

The Entrepreneur's Journey: A small business owner shifted from stressing over competition and profit margins to focusing on service, collaboration, and community. By trusting that there was enough success for everyone, he attracted unexpected partnerships—and his business experienced exponential growth.

The Family's Transformation: A family going through financial struggles chose to shift their focus—from what they lacked to what they had: love, laughter, and one another. This new perspective brought them closer together and inspired creative solutions they wouldn't have otherwise seen. They began to view their home not through the lens of scarcity, but as a space full of connection, warmth, and potential.

Abundance begins with the way we choose to see the world. When we shift our perspective, embrace generosity, and trust in possibility, we open ourselves to a life filled with creativity, connection, and unexpected opportunities.

In the illustrations above, do you see how shifting focus from scarcity to abundance created new opportunities? _____

If so, is there one area of life where a mindset shift might bring abundance?

SUSTAINING ABUNDANCE

Living abundantly isn't a one-time decision—it's a continuous practice rooted in intention and self-awareness. Like any worthwhile pursuit, maintaining an abundance mindset involves consistent effort to stay aligned with your values and goals. It means regularly pausing to reflect on your progress, celebrating milestones along the way, and remaining open to opportunities that may not initially seem obvious.

Gratitude is the foundation of abundance. It grounds you in the richness of the present while keeping your heart open to future possibilities. By nurturing these habits, you'll not only sustain abundance in your life but also deepen your connection to it, creating a lasting sense of joy, fulfillment, and growth.

Regular Reflection: Set aside time each week to reflect on your abundance journey. Journal about recent experiences, review your goals, or sit quietly with your thoughts. Ask yourself: *"Where did I notice abundance this week?"* or *"What area of my life needs more attention right now?"*
Reflection helps you track growth, realign with your intentions, and celebrate the changes you've made. It turns your progress into a conscious, empowering practice.

Celebrate Milestones: Every achievement—big or small—deserves to be celebrated, reminds you of how far you've come, and fuels your enthusiasm for what's next. Take time to truly appreciate these wins. Treat yourself, share your success with loved ones, or document the achievement in your journal. Celebrations build momentum and encourage you to keep moving forward with confidence and enthusiasm.

Stay Open: Abundance doesn't always look the way you expect. Stay open to new paths, new people, and new ideas. Often, the opportunities that lead to the most growth and joy arrive in unexpected packages.

For example, I was once invited to be part of a reality TV show. My first reaction? *"No way."* But after reflecting and journaling, **I decided to say yes**—and that yes opened doors I never could've imagined. The friendships, personal growth, and experiences that followed became an unforgettable part of my abundance journey.

Practice Gratitude: I've mentioned this over and over again: gratitude is the cornerstone of abundance. Make it a daily practice to focus on the good in your life, whether it's through writing in a gratitude journal, sharing your appreciation with others, or simply pausing to notice and acknowledge moments of beauty. Gratitude shifts your focus from what you lack to what you have, reinforcing an abundance mindset. Over time, this habit trains your mind to see more of the positive, creating a ripple effect that enhances every area of your life.

By integrating these practices into your daily life, you can sustain the abundance you've worked to cultivate, ensuring it continues to grow and thrive. These habits don't just strengthen your mindset—they build the foundation for a life rooted in joy, peace, and purpose. The more you commit to them, the more natural it becomes to live abundantly, every single day.

Do you recognize that sustaining abundance requires a daily investment of time and energy? _____

If so, write down how much time—realistically—you're willing to invest each day to support your abundance mindset. (5 minutes? 15? An hour?)

_____

_____

_____

What's one abundance practice you'll commit to starting with now?

_____

_____

_____

STEPPING INTO ABUNDANCE

Your abundant life is already within reach—waiting for you to claim it, step into it, and live it fully. If you've made it this far, it means something inside you already knows: you're ready. You've already taken important steps toward shifting your perspective, embracing gratitude, and opening yourself to the universe's infinite possibilities. Now, it's time to fully step into your power and say yes to the abundance that's already trying to reach you.

By shifting your mindset, aligning your actions, and embracing gratitude, you open the door to a life filled with joy, purpose, and prosperity. Abundance isn't just something you achieve—it's a way of being. **In this sense, abundance acts as both a verb and a noun.** Each intentional step you take toward living abundantly moves you closer to your highest potential and a life that is truly rich in every sense of the word.

Step boldly into your abundant life, confident that even more awaits you. Now that you've explored what an abundant life can truly look and feel like…

Do you feel like you've gained a deeper understanding of what an abundant life can truly feel like? _____

Revisit your definition of abundance. Has it shifted or expanded since the start of this chapter? _____
If so, write down what abundance means to you now—and how you'll live into that definition moving forward.

_____

_____

_____

_____

Abundance Manifestation Practices

TURNING DREAMS INTO REALITY

Once, in the quiet coastal village of Aveiro, on the western shore of Portugal, lived a woman named Lira who dreamed of weaving sails for great ships. Not ordinary sails—she wanted to craft the kind that would carry explorers to distant lands, that would dance with the wind and transform the dreams of voyagers into motion.

Her dream, however, was born from hardship.

Years earlier, her husband—a kind and quiet fisherman—had died in a sudden storm off the island of Ilha de São Miguel. The sea that had once been a source of joy and livelihood became a place of grief. Left to raise their two little daughters alone, Lira took whatever work she could find—mending nets, repairing sails, sewing worn clothing for other sailors' wives. Every job kept her close to the water, and closer still to the memory of the man she loved.

But her heart still longed for something more. She imagined a life where she could create—not just survive.

So she dreamed. And she drew.

She poured her vision into a journal, filling it with sketches—hundreds, even thousands over the years—of sails and knots, colored fibers and boats of every kind. Each page became a whispered promise to herself and her daughters. The journal was her blueprint, her meditation, her emotional compass.

Villagers admired her strength but often called her a dreamer.

"Wishing won't make it so," they said.

But Lira didn't just wish—she prepared.

She studied the way the wind moved, how fabric caught and curved. She learned about tension, durability, and balance. She bartered for scraps, spun fibers from wild flax, and repaired old canvas in exchange for knowledge. Every day, she took a small action that aligned with the vision she carried in her heart.

Years passed. Her daughters grew. One spring, a fierce storm swept through the coast, destroying many of the sails in the harbor. With no time to wait for deliveries from Lisbon or beyond, the ship captains turned to the village—and to Lira.

She worked day and night, weaving with the precision of someone who had lived this moment a thousand times in her mind. Her sails held strong, and word of her work spread to harbors far beyond Aveiro.

She provided wonderfully for her daughters—a warm home filled with laughter, a thriving business they would one day follow her into, and a legacy built not just on thread and canvas, but on vision, faith, and perseverance.

And when asked how she had done it, Lira simply smiled and said:

"I didn't just dream. I aligned my dream—with love, belief, vision, and action. And when the wind finally came, I was ready to rise with it."

Manifestation is not about waiting for the wind—it's about weaving the sails. And if you're wise, you'll sketch the dream, color it with feeling, and prepare for its arrival—even before the breeze begins to blow.

But dreaming, feeling, and preparing are only part of the equation. While often confused with wishful thinking, true manifestation is an intentional practice—one that blends deep belief, clear vision, aligned emotion, and consistent action.

At the center of it all is belief—not just in your dreams, but in your capacity to achieve them. A grounded, quiet knowing that what you are creating is possible—and already unfolding. Because without that inner conviction, it's easy to give up just before the miracle arrives.

It's not magic. It's intentionally moving through life with purpose, clarity, and aligned action—toward what you truly believe will help you love your life. It's doing the internal work so that your external world becomes a reflection of your deepest truth and your most courageous desires.

In this chapter, you'll explore the principles behind this practice, understand how it connects to *Perceptual Shifting*, and engage in exercises that help you manifest with greater clarity, consistency, and success.

By the end, you'll have a comprehensive toolkit for turning your visions into reality—and a deeper understanding of how to live in alignment with your most abundant and empowered self.

Do you believe you can manifest more successfully by aligning your dreams with both belief and action? _____

If so, think of something you'd like to manifest—whether it's a relationship, a financial goal, a creative pursuit, or even a move. Write it down, list the specific actions you can take, and describe the mindset that will best support your success.

_____

_____

_____

_____

_____

_____

_____

THE SCIENCE BEHIND MANIFESTATION

Manifestation is grounded in psychological and neurological principles, one of which is the Reticular Activating System (RAS)—a network of neurons extending from the midbrain to the medulla. This part of your brain acts as a filter, processing the millions of bits of information you encounter daily and focusing your attention on what matters most to you. Essentially, the RAS highlights what you believe is important.

The RAS plays a pivotal role in shaping your reality by emphasizing what you consciously or subconsciously focus on. If you frequently think, *"My life is a mess,"* the RAS directs your mind to notice evidence supporting that belief. Conversely, when you affirm, *"I love my life,"* the RAS accentuates the positive aspects of your experience. This filtering system is why your thoughts and self-talk are so powerful in influencing your perspective and outcomes.

To illustrate, imagine you decide to buy a red car. Suddenly, you begin noticing red cars everywhere. Your brain didn't create more red cars; it simply prioritized information to align with your focus. Understanding how the RAS works empowers you to create a *Perceptual Shift* by aligning your focus with your goals and desires. Try putting some of the following exercises into action to harness this potential.

- *Visualize Your Goals:* Spend time daily vividly imagining your goals as if you've already achieved them. See, hear, and feel the details to make them real in your mind.

- *Set Clear Intentions:* Write down specific, actionable goals that align with what you desire. The more precise you are, the easier it is for your RAS to filter opportunities related to your goal.

- *Affirm Your Beliefs:* Use positive affirmations to reinforce what you want. For example, "I attract opportunities that align with my purpose."

- *Reticular Reflection:* Review how you directed your focus each day.

Celebrate moments when you consciously shifted your RAS toward positivity or growth, and note any opportunities for improvement.

Neuroplasticity: The brain's remarkable ability to adapt, grow, and form new neural connections based on your thoughts, habits, and experiences. You have the power to rewire your brain for success and positivity.

Repeated thoughts and actions strengthen neural pathways, making those patterns more automatic over time. Negative thought patterns can be replaced with positive ones through consistent effort. Here's how to use it:

- *Positive Visualization:* Imagine the life you want in detail. Picture yourself achieving your goals, experiencing joy, and overcoming challenges.

- *Practice Affirmations.* State positive affirmations daily while vividly imagining yourself achieving your goals and experiencing joy. Pairing affirmations with visualization ingrains them in your subconscious, guiding your mindset and actions. Begin each morning with three affirmations and spend five minutes visualizing your desired outcomes before bed.

- *Break Negative Patterns:* Identify limiting beliefs or negative thought patterns and consciously replace them with empowering thoughts.

Emotion and Energy: Your emotions create a vibrational frequency that interacts with the world around you. Positive emotions like gratitude, joy, and excitement emit a high frequency, which, according to the Law of Attraction, draws similar energies and experiences into your life.

Frequently the term *"higher power"* is associated with universal consciousness, God, or another spiritual force. However, in this context, it's about tapping into the higher, more loving frequency of life—the elevated energy that arises from gratitude, compassion, and joy.

It's a shift from a *"lower power"* fueled by fear, anger, or scarcity, to aligning with the positive, abundant energy that creates and attracts growth, healing, connection and love.

Plugging into this higher power isn't about religious belief; it's about embracing the higher version of yourself and the world you want to live in. Think of this higher power as a state of love, kindness and good, versus the lower power of selfishness, anger and victimization.

Cultivate Positive Emotions: People who love their lives and live in the Attitude of Gratitude naturally attract abundance because they focus on what they have rather than what they lack. Here are some actions you can take to foster this mindset:

- *Practice Gratitude:* Begin and end each day by writing down three things you're grateful for, no matter how small.

- *Feel the Emotion:* When you visualize or affirm, focus not just on the thought but on the emotion tied to it—feel the joy, gratitude, or excitement as if your desire is already fulfilled.

- *Surround Yourself with Positive Energy:* Spend time with uplifting people, consume inspiring content, and engage in activities that bring you joy.

- *Manifestation Manual:* In your journal to track the feelings, thoughts, and desires you wish to manifest in your life. Regularly reflect on how these desires evolve and celebrate when they come to fruition. By observing this process, you reinforce the power of intentional focus, cultivating deeper gratitude for the abundance that unfolds.

- *Express Gratitude to Others*: Make it a habit to acknowledge and appreciate the people in your life. A simple thank-you note, compliment, or act of kindness strengthens connections and amplifies the positive energy you put out into the world.

By understanding and applying the principles of the RAS, neuroplasticity, and the power of emotion and energy, you create a powerful framework for aligning your thoughts, habits, and actions with the life you desire. Incorporate these tools into your daily routine and watch how you're able to manifest opportunities, growth, and abundance as they unfold naturally.

ABUNDANCE MANIFESTATION PRACTICES

Do you see how aligning your thoughts, emotions, and actions can rewire your brain and train your focus toward abundance? _____

Here is one goal I will visualize now:

_____

With regard to that goal, here is my intention:

_____

I will affirm my belief that I can achieve it by reciting the following affirmation out loud each day:

_____

I will stop engaging in the following negative habit that sabotages my ability to achieve this goal:

_____

I will attempt to review and reflect each day on how well I followed through with my affirmations and intentions, celebrating progress on this goal.

Check the following box that statement is true: ☐

I will do my best to practice gratitude each day for both having this goal and the efforts I am making to achieve it.

Check the following box that statement is true: ☐

I will encourage others in their goals and spend time people who both encourage me and believe in my ability to achieve this goal.

Check the following box that statement is true: ☐

I will track my progress toward this goal in my journal.

Check the following box that statement is true: ☐

THE PILLARS OF MANIFESTATION

Manifestation is not a magical process; it's a deliberate practice of aligning your thoughts, beliefs, and actions to create the life you desire. To succeed, it requires a foundation rooted in specific principles—each one a critical piece of the puzzle. By embracing these pillars, you ensure that your manifestation efforts are purposeful, balanced, and deeply effective.

Clarity: Be specific about what you want. Vague goals lead to vague results because your mind and energy are scattered.

Imagine telling a waiter, "I'll have food," versus ordering your favorite meal.

The clearer you are, the easier it becomes for your mind to focus and for opportunities to present themselves. Visualize every detail of what you desire—what it looks like, feels like, and the emotions it brings you.

Belief: Trust in your ability to achieve your desires and in the universe's abundance. Earlier in this book, we explored the word "faith" and how, in this context, it translates to belief—the voice that says, "Everything is going to work out," rather than the fearful whisper of, "No, it's not."

Belief is the engine that powers manifestation; without it, doubt seeps in and derails your focus. Strengthen your belief by affirming your worthiness daily and reflecting on past successes as evidence that you can create the outcomes you seek. When you trust that abundance is limitless and available, you open the door to invite it into your life.

Action: Manifestation is not a passive daydream—it requires consistent effort toward your goals. Taking even small, deliberate steps daily signals your commitment to the universe and reinforces your belief in yourself. Whether it's making a call, researching your goal, or improving a skill, action transforms your dreams into tangible results. *After all, no one ever filled their refrigerator by simply wishing from the couch.*

ABUNDANCE MANIFESTATION PRACTICES

Gratitude: Cultivate an attitude of appreciation for what you have and what's to come. Gratitude shifts your focus from lack to abundance, opening your eyes to the opportunities already present in your life. Express gratitude for progress, no matter how small, and for the future manifestations that are yet to come. This attitude keeps your energy positive and attracts more reasons to be thankful.

Detach from Results: Release the desire to control the outcome and trust the process. Detachment doesn't mean giving up on your goals—it means letting go of the anxiety and desperation that often accompany the pursuit of desires. When you accept outcomes that may not align with your desires, trust the timing of the universe and focus on the fact that you did, or you are doing, your part. Allow things to unfold naturally, and often they will in ways better than you imagined. *Trust that wherever the sails carry you, it will be exactly where you're meant to go.*

Manifestation thrives on balance. It requires clarity to define your goals, belief to trust in their achievement, action to set the wheels in motion, gratitude to sustain positive energy, and detachment from outcomes to allow space for growth. When all these pillars are in place, you create a harmonious flow that aligns your inner world with your external reality. By embracing these principles, you can manifest not just your dreams, but a life rich in purpose, joy, and abundance.

Do you understand why all five pillars of manifestation—Clarity, Belief, Action, Gratitude, and Detachment—create the foundation for lasting abundance? _____

If so, which of these pillars do you feel most confident in, and which one do you think you need to strengthen? Write one small step you can take today to reinforce the pillar that needs the most attention.

_____

_____

_____

OVERCOMING MANIFESTATION BLOCKS

Manifestation isn't just about setting intentions—it requires aligning thoughts, emotions, and actions while clearing the blocks that hold you back. Here are some of the most common manifestation obstacles:

Avoid Negative Programming: Self-sabotaging thoughts—those deep-seated beliefs, self-doubt, and limiting thoughts—can act as significant blocks to manifestation. These mental habits, often rooted in past experiences or societal conditioning, cloud your vision, undermine your confidence, and limit your potential to attract abundance. Recognizing and addressing this programming is essential to shifting your mindset and aligning with your desires.

As you dismantle mental blocks, affirmations become a powerful tool for transformation. By replacing negative thoughts with positive statements, you retrain your mind to focus on possibilities, build self-worth, and align your energy with the reality you want to create. Affirmations disrupt negative patterns and reinforce the belief that you are capable, deserving, and ready to manifest your dreams.

One of my favorites is, "I love my life!" At first, I spoke it as an intention, wanting to truly feel it. Now, I say it often because I genuinely do. I wholeheartedly believe that the words you speak out loud have the power to shape your reality. By consistently affirming what you desire, you align your thoughts, emotions, and actions with the life you want to create.

Avoid Impossible Goals: A common block in manifestation involves setting goals that are too broad or overwhelming. When your desires feel massive and undefined—like "I want to be successful" or "I want to change my life"—they can lead to confusion, inaction, and frustration. Overarching goals often lack clarity and direction, making it difficult to determine where to begin or how to measure progress.

To overcome this block, focus on breaking your goals into smaller, actionable steps. Instead of aiming for "success," identify what success looks like to you and outline the specific actions needed to achieve it. For example, if your goal is financial abundance, start by creating a budget, saving a set amount each month, or researching investment opportunities.

Smaller steps provide clarity, build momentum, and make large goals feel achievable. Each completed task is a milestone, reinforcing your belief in your ability to manifest your desires and keeping you aligned with your vision. By taking it one step at a time, you transform overwhelming ambitions into a clear path forward.

Use your journal as a tool to write down your goals and break them into manageable steps, refining and adjusting as required. Alternatively, take advantage of tools on your smartphone or laptop, such as task management apps or digital notes, to track and organize your steps.

One of the biggest challenges people face with goals is making them too big or setting too many at once, which can quickly become overwhelming. To avoid this, try the following:

- *Start Small:* Focus on one primary goal at a time and break it into smaller, achievable tasks. For example, if your goal is to write a book, start with a single chapter or even a paragraph a day.

- *Prioritize:* List your tasks in order of importance and tackle the most critical ones first. This helps you build momentum and keeps your focus clear.

- *Set Timelines:* Assign realistic deadlines to your steps to create a sense of accountability and progress without unnecessary pressure.

- *Celebrate Progress:* Acknowledge and celebrate completing even the smallest tasks—it reinforces your commitment and boosts motivation.

- *Stay Flexible:* Goals and circumstances can change. Be open to refining your plan without losing sight of your ultimate desire.

By keeping your steps small and focused, you transform daunting goals into manageable actions, reducing overwhelm and increasing success. Affirmations like 'I'm open to financial abundance' help shift your mindset, but when combined with concrete steps—like budgeting or saving—they become a catalyst for real change.

Don't Ignore Your Gut: One major block to manifestation is dismissing or second-guessing your inner voice—your intuition. Ignoring your gut instincts often stems from overthinking, self-doubt, or relying too heavily on logic alone. Sometimes we do this as the result of feeling influenced by others. This can lead to missed opportunities or decisions that don't align with your authentic goals and values.

Pay attention to the subtle nudges, ideas, or opportunities that resonate with you and feel aligned with your goals and values. Intuition is a powerful inner guide that often leads you toward the right decisions and opportunities when you trust it. Here's how to harness and act on your intuition:

- *Quiet Your Mind:* Spend time in meditation, mindfulness, or quiet reflection to tune out external noise and connect with your inner voice. A calm mind is better able to recognize intuitive signals.

- *Notice Patterns and Feelings:* Intuition often manifests as recurring thoughts, feelings, or a sense of knowing. Pay attention to these signs and how they resonate with your goals or current circumstances.

- *Trust the Gut Feeling:* When something feels "right" or "off," trust your instincts. Your subconscious mind often picks up on details and insights that your conscious mind might overlook. **If a choice isn't rooted in love—for yourself and others—it may lead to fear, confusion, or unintended pain.**

- *Act Quickly on Aligned Ideas:* When you feel inspired, take action. Intuition often comes as a fleeting thought or opportunity—seize it before fear or doubt creeps in. If you can't act immediately, write it down in your journal or send yourself a quick text to capture the idea. This ensures your inspiration doesn't slip away and allows you to return to it when you're ready to take action.

- *Try Your Ideas—Let Go of Fear:* Test your intuitive ideas by taking small, measured risks. No risk, no reward—each step forward provides clarity and momentum. Remember, there are no true mistakes or failures—only stepping stones guiding you toward abundance. The more you act, the more you refine your path and strengthen your trust in yourself.

- *Avoid Overanalyzing:* While logical analysis has its place, intuition works best when you don't second-guess it. Overthinking can drown out the quiet voice of your inner guidance. When you see every experience as growth rather than failure, you free yourself to trust the process and move forward with confidence.

- *Surround Yourself with Supportive Energy:* Intuition thrives in positive environments. Spend time with people who encourage your growth and trust your instincts rather than doubting or dismissing them. It's okay to keep your ideas to yourself until they're strong enough to stand on their own.

By following your intuition, you align with opportunities and decisions that feel authentic and true to your path, creating a smoother and more fulfilling journey toward your goals.

Stay Consistent: Manifestation thrives on steady effort and commitment. Build momentum by taking daily steps, no matter how small. When challenges arise, adjust rather than quit. Consistency strengthens focus, reinforces belief, and keeps you aligned with your desires.

However, it's important to remember that falling off track doesn't mean failure—it's part of being human. What matters most is your ability to recognize when you've veered off course and to recommit to your goals. Instead of judging yourself harshly, view these moments as opportunities to practice resilience and refocus.

Regular effort is the foundation of progress, building momentum and keeping you on track toward your goals. Consistency doesn't mean perfection—it's about showing up and taking small, intentional steps every day, even when motivation wanes. Here are ways to stay consistent and make steady progress:

- *Establish a Routine:* Create a daily or weekly schedule that includes time dedicated to working on your goals. A predictable routine helps turn effort into habit.

- *Create Accountability:* Share your goals with a trusted friend, mentor, or group who can help keep you accountable and provide encouragement.

- *Embrace Imperfection:* Consistency doesn't mean you'll always be able to shift perceptions every time you recognize it might be beneficial. Nor does it mean you'll live in a constant state of enlightenment. Focus on progress, not perfection. Lighten up, and don't take setbacks too seriously—embrace a sense of humor about them, as they're a natural part of growth.

- *Revisit Your Why:* Regularly remind yourself why you're pursuing your goals. A clear sense of purpose can reignite your commitment when challenges arise.

Impatience: When things don't go your way, it's easy to feel frustrated and ask, *Why can't I have this now?* or *Why isn't this happening for me?* Impatience stems from a desire to control outcomes, a belief that things should unfold on your timeline rather than in timing of the universe. But forcing things before their time can create resistance, stress, and even push what you desire further away.

Impatience often brings anger, frustration, and doubt—questioning whether the universe is truly working in your favor. But manifestation isn't about demanding instant results; it's about aligning with life's flow. The more you try to force things, the more you block what's meant for you. Here are some ways to shift out of impatience when you feel it arise:

- *Pause & Reflect:* When impatience arises, ask yourself, What am I afraid will happen if this doesn't happen now? Often, impatience masks fear or lack of trust.

- *Trust the Timing:* Just because something isn't happening yet doesn't mean it isn't happening at all. The best things often arrive at the perfect moment—not necessarily when we demand them.

- *Let Go of the 'How' & 'When':* Focus on what you want, but release attachment to when and how it unfolds. Your job is alignment, not micromanaging the universe.

- *Replace Frustration with Faith:* Every delay, redirection, or closed door is either protecting you or preparing you for something better. Instead of resisting, trust that life is unfolding for your highest good.

Patience isn't about waiting idly—it's about trusting, allowing, and knowing that what's meant for you will not pass you by. When you let go of the desperate need for control, you make space for miracles to unfold.

Self-Doubt: Overcoming self-doubt begins with intentionally building your confidence by acknowledging your strengths and past achievements.

Reflect on and celebrate the challenges you've overcome and the successes you've achieved, no matter how small. These moments are proof of your resilience, capabilities, and progress, and serve as reminders that you are capable of overcoming all obstacles and achieving your goals.

Instead of letting failures fuel self-doubt, view them as opportunities for growth that prepare you for future challenges. Acknowledge and celebrate every achievement, no matter how small. This reinforces your confidence and reminds you of your ability to succeed.

Another way to help overcome self-doubt is to do some mirror work every morning. Look into your eyes and tell yourself how proud you are of your accomplishments, the way you're evolving, and how you're turning obstacles into opportunities. And be sure you say I love you, followed by your name, and looking into your eyes. Even if it feels silly at first, keep trying anyway.

You may be surprised by how powerful it feels to speak kindly to yourself.

Confidence isn't built overnight—it's a gradual process of shifting your mindset, embracing your strengths, and trusting in your ability to navigate life's challenges. By focusing on your past successes and affirming your abilities daily, you'll transform self-doubt into self-assurance and open the door to greater possibilities.

Fear of Failure: This common obstacle to growth often sabotages progress and keeps us stuck in a cycle of inaction. It can manifest as procrastination, perfectionism, self-doubt, or a refusal to take risks, paralyzing us with the worry of making the wrong choices, being wrong, letting others down, or facing judgment.

This mindset, often rooted in past experiences or societal expectations, can make failure feel like something to be avoided at all costs, this mindset can feel like a liability. However, by reframing failure as a natural and valuable part of growth, we free ourselves from its grip and gain the courage to move forward. In fact, failure—when embraced—becomes a powerful teacher. Here's how the fear of failure, without a *Perceptual Shift*, can hold us back:

- *Procrastination:* The fear of not doing something perfectly can lead us to delay or avoid starting altogether. Often times the longer we wait, the harder it is to get started.

- *Perfectionism:* Setting unrealistically high standards keeps us from finishing or even attempting tasks because we're afraid of falling short. It's important to remember that perfection is unattainable, and striving for it only holds us back. Our best *is* always good enough.

- *Self-Sabotage:* Fear of failure can lead us to undermine our own efforts by abandoning projects before completion or not trying at all, convincing ourselves it's better not to try than to risk failing.

- *Overthinking:* Constantly analyzing potential outcomes can leave us stuck in indecision and prevent us from taking action. It's like running on a hamster wheel—exhausting and gets us nowhere. Instead, try writing down your thoughts to clear your mind, and either take action or wait until inspiration strikes.

- **Limiting Beliefs:** Distorted perceptions and restricted thoughts can block manifestation. Identify and reframe these thoughts to align with your vision by writing down any doubts or fears related to your goals. Next to each limiting belief, replace it with an empowering one that uplifts and motivates you.

For example, transform:

> *"I'll get it done tomorrow"* to *"I'll spend 10 minutes on this today."*
>
> *"I'll share once I'm an expert"* to *"I'll do my best and get feedback."*
>
> *"This must be perfect"* to *"I'm learning, it need not be perfect."*
>
> *"I'm not good enough,"* to *"I am capable and deserving of success."*
>
> *"I'm not attractive,"* to *"I am beautiful and radiate confidence."*

- **Avoidance of Risk:** Fear of failure can cause us to play close to the vest, avoiding opportunities that might push us out of our comfort zone. Never forget that the most successful individuals got there by taking risks. Spend time every day getting out of your comfort zone.

Clearing the blocks to manifestation requires awareness, intentional action, and a willingness to shift deeply ingrained patterns. By replacing negative programming with empowering beliefs, breaking overwhelming goals into manageable steps, trusting your intuition, and staying consistent, you create a foundation for attracting abundance with greater ease.

Letting go of impatience, self-doubt, and fear of failure allows you to align with the natural flow of life, transforming obstacles into stepping stones. As you move forward with clarity, confidence, and trust in your path, manifestation becomes less about struggle and more about allowing what is already meant for you to unfold.

THE PERCEPTUAL SHIFT

Do you recognize any of the manifestation blocks discussed in this chapter—such as fear of failure, impatience, self-doubt, or negative programming—showing up in your life? _____

What is one thing you've been wanting to manifest in your life that hasn't come to fruition yet? Write it down.

_____

_____

_____

_____

What specific block—or blocks—do you feel have held you back from manifesting it? Be honest and specific.

_____

_____

_____

_____

What tools or practices can you use to release those blocks and allow the abundance you deserve to flow more freely into your life?

_____

_____

_____

_____

FINDING SUCCESS IN FAILURE

Failure is often viewed as something to avoid, but in reality, it is one of the greatest teachers in life. Every misstep, setback, or unexpected outcome presents an opportunity to grow. When you shift your perception of failure from something negative to a stepping stone toward success, you release fear, embrace resilience, and open yourself up to unlimited possibilities.

Think of it this way: How could you possibly master math without making mistakes along the way? Failure isn't the opposite of success—it's the path to it. Here are ways to reframe failure so that when it happens—and it will—you'll be lifted by it rather than weighed down. Here's how we can turn our lemons into lemonade:

- *Shift Your Perspective:* Learn to recognize that failure isn't the opposite of success—it's a step toward it. Failures are actually building blocks helping to refine your approach and prepare you for future challenges. Remember, some of the biggest "failures" turned out to be the biggest successes.

- *Detach Your Worth:* Recognize that your value as a person is not tied to external validation, successes, or outside appearances. Often, we seek approval from others to feel worthy, but this reliance can make us overly dependent on their opinions. Your value comes from who you are, not what you achieve or how others perceive you

  Remember, failure is simply feedback—a stepping stone for growth—making you smarter and more capable. Instead of *"failing at doing it,"* you actually *"learned how not to do it."*

- *Celebrate Effort:* Every attempt, even if it results in failure, is a victory because it's an opportunity to grow. Remember, you don't have to hit a home run every time you step up to the plate—what matters is that you're willing to step up and swing. Celebrating the courage it took to try reinforces your willingness to get up and try again.

THE PERCEPTUAL SHIFT

- *Learn from Mistakes:* Reflect on what went wrong, identify areas for improvement, and adjust your strategy. Treat failure as a wonderful opportunity to try a new approach rather than the end of a journey.

- *Practice Self-Compassion:* Be kind to yourself when you stumble. Rather than being overly critical, offer yourself the same encouragement you would give a friend learning something new. Remember, self-compassion is a vital part of growth!

- *Redefine Success:* Expand your definition of success to include learning, growth, and persistence—not just the end result. In a word, it's about "evolution." With every endeavor you embark about, you're growing into a richer and wiser version of yourself.

Reframing failure as growth allows you to approach life with confidence and curiosity rather than fear and hesitation. Each experience, whether it goes as planned or not, contributes to your evolution. The key isn't avoiding failure—it's using it as fuel for success. When you truly embrace this, you'll begin to welcome failure as a path towards success, and in doing so, you'll be fully living in *The Perceptual Shift*.

Do you generally view your failures in a negative light? _____

Think of an experience where something didn't go as planned and you still view it in a negative way. Write in detail about what happened, how it made you feel, and why it still feels like a failure.

_____

_____

_____

Now, shift your perspective and write out how this experience be seen as a stepping stone rather than a setback.

_____

_____

Now, write about one valuable lesson you learned going through the experience.

_____
_____
_____

Now, write about how—had this never happened—what opportunity, growth, or wisdom you might have missed.

_____
_____
_____

If you've been feeling unsuccessful in any way as a result of this experience, list one thing that actually makes you more successful as a person for having gone through it.

_____
_____
_____

Now, write a new statement about this experience—one that frames it as part of your growth, not your defeat. Instead of starting the statement with "I failed," try starting it with "As a result of this experience, I learned that."

_____
_____
_____
_____

- *Turning Lemons into Lemonade*: Do this same exercise for any other past failures that still feel heavy. With each shift, you'll find more freedom, wisdom, and resilience.

TRANSCENDING FEAR OF FAILURE

Overcoming the fear of failure requires shifting from avoidance to growth and resilience. Failure isn't a dead-end or something to be feared—it's one of your greatest teachers. By taking small, intentional steps, surrounding yourself with support, and celebrating failures as progress, you build the confidence to take on bigger challenges. The goal isn't to avoid failure—it's to learn, adapt, and keep moving forward, knowing that each setback brings you closer to your potential.

- *Visualizing Positive Outcomes:* Focus on what success looks and feels like to cultivate a sense of possibility and excitement. Stay flexible—things might not go as planned, but they could also turn out even better than you imagined. Spencer Silver, in his efforts to create a super-strong adhesive, created a super-weak one. He repurposed it and created Post-it® Notes, which was a huge success.

- *Embracing 'Good Enough':* Let go of perfectionism and focus on progress rather than perfection. Remember, humility is a strength, and *'good enough'* often paves the way for growth and success. Instead of saying, "I didn't achieve my goal," try *"that's a good start"*.

- *Document the Growth:* Write down your perceived failures, the lessons they've taught you, and the ways they've contributed to your growth. This practice transforms failure into an opportunity for learning, fostering a mindset of resilience and abundance that allows you to see value in every experience. Examples of this can be found in **The Perceptual Shift Journal**.

- *Surrounding Yourself with Support:* Spend time with people who encourage you to take risks and view setbacks as part of life's process. There will always be plenty of people to doubt you or put you down, and sometimes we can use this for motivation. But the best motivators are those who believe in you, I call them our *"cheerleaders"*.

- *Taking Action Quickly:* The longer you wait, the more your fear can grow.

Commit to taking the first step, even if it's small, as each action you take diminishes fear's power over you. Just like a runner who's not in the mood to run knows that putting on their running shoes is the most powerful step they can take to work up a sweat.

Speaking of powerful first steps, reading this book is one you've already taken toward overcoming your fears. Each time you use one of the tools inside, you'll be taking another. With every new habit you adopt, every difficult conversation you approach differently, and every opportunity you say yes to, you'll build momentum and strengthen your courage.

By reframing failure as a natural part of growth and adopting a mindset of curiosity and resilience, you free yourself from its paralyzing effects. Instead of seeing failure as something to avoid, you'll begin to view it as an essential and transformative step on the path to your success.

Attachment to Outcomes: Living with rigid expectations often leads to disappointment and resentment when things don't turn out as planned. **It's often said that expectations are the breeding ground for resentment**.

Instead of wanting, needing, or obsessing over specific results, focus on doing your best and trusting the universe to unfold things in a way that serves your highest good. More often than not, letting go of the reins leads to unexpected abundance—even when things don't go "your way."

By surrendering expectations and embracing the journey, you free yourself to fully experience the present moment, noticing the gifts you weren't expecting. This shift allows you to evolve into an even more wonderful version of yourself while creating space for unexpected opportunities and growth.

Overcoming Overwhelm: When life feels overwhelming, it's easy to get caught in a cycle of stress—juggling responsibilities, caring for others, and managing endless tasks. I call this **"piling"**—taking on too much at once, leaving little room for clarity, balance, or progress.

Imagine being at Thanksgiving and, instead of trying a few dishes and coming back for seconds, you pile your plate with everything at once, overflowing it. There's a good chance that something delicious—perhaps even the tastiest thing being served—ends up falling onto the floor, wasted.

Rushing through everything at once also doesn't serve you or those around you—it robs you of the present moment and keeps you stuck in frustration, stress, and exhaustion. When we become human doings instead of human beings, it's a sign to pause, take a deep breath, and realign with intention. In order to shift out of overwhelm:

- *Do One Thing at a Time:* Multitasking can scatter your energy. Prioritize tasks, focus on what matters most, and tackle them one by one.
- *Let Go of Control:* You don't have to force everything into place. Trust that things will unfold as they're meant to.
- *Stay Present:* Overwhelm often comes from worrying about the past or future. Ground yourself in the here and now.

Growth and transformation rarely happen on a predictable schedule. The process *is just as important as the destination*—and sometimes, the delays and detours are what shape you most. By releasing stress and surrendering to life's natural flow—*trusting the timing of your journey*—you create space for clarity, ease, and joy.

Is there an area of your life you regret not pursuing because of a fear of failure or the belief that you just couldn't do it? _____

If so, write about that missed opportunity in detail. What was it, why did you hesitate, and how did fear hold you back?

_____

_____

_____

_____

ABUNDANCE MANIFESTATION PRACTICES

Now, imagine what could have happened if you had taken the leap. How might your life be different today?

_____

_____

_____

_____

_____

What would you tell your past self about fear and failure, knowing what you now understand?

_____

_____

_____

_____

_____

Finally, write one commitment to yourself about how you will approach opportunities differently moving forward.

_____

_____

_____

_____

_____

_____

HOW GRATITUDE FUELS MANIFESTATION

Gratitude amplifies manifestation by directing your energy toward the abundance already present in your life. Here's how to practice it:

Gratitude Journaling: Write down at least three things you're grateful for each day, including progress toward your goals. *The Perceptual Shift Journal* provides ideas and examples to guide your practice. Let's try it now:

Write down 3 things you're grateful for:

_____

_____

_____

Express Appreciation: Each day, take a moment to thank the people who support you. Whether it's a heartfelt note, a thoughtful gift, a simple text, or even a quiet word of gratitude to yourself, expressing appreciation strengthens relationships, uplifts others, and deepens your own sense of abundance. Small acts of gratitude can create a powerful ripple effect, fostering connection and positivity for both you and those around you. Let's try it now:

List three people you're grateful for:

_____

_____

_____

Celebrate Small Wins: Recognize and celebrate every step forward. Each achievement, no matter how small, builds momentum, reinforces positive habits, and reminds you of your progress toward larger goals. Even making your bed, completing a task, or sticking to a routine is worth celebrating. Let's try it now.

ABUNDANCE MANIFESTATION PRACTICES

Write down three achievements you've made in the last week:

_____

_____

_____

Gratitude and manifestation work hand in hand to create a powerful cycle of abundance. When you focus on what you're grateful for, you amplify it—your mind acts like a magnifying glass, making what you appreciate grow larger in your experience.

But gratitude isn't just about recognizing what's already present; it's about acknowledging the steps you're taking to manifest more. As you shift your perceptions, strengthen your belief in your ability to create, and actively engage in manifestation practices like affirmations and visualization, you align yourself with greater abundance.

Celebrating your progress—whether it's a subtle mindset shift, an opportunity you attracted, or a deepened sense of joy—reinforces your belief in your ability to manifest. The more you recognize and appreciate what you're creating, the stronger your manifestation muscle becomes, allowing abundance to flow even more freely into your life.

Do you see how gratitude not only amplifies what you already have but also strengthens your ability to manifest more? _____

Fill in the blanks in the following statement then read it aloud.

"I am grateful for _____,

_____, and _____, and as

I continue to focus on abundance, I welcome more _____,

_____, and _____ into my life."

ADVANCED MANIFESTATION TECHNIQUES

The most successful manifesters go beyond basic practices, dedicating time and effort to techniques that deepen their alignment with abundance. While many people set intentions or visualize their desires occasionally, true transformation happens when these practices become a consistent, intentional part of daily life.

Methods like vision boards, scripting, meditation, and energy clearing require patience and take commitment, but they yield profound results—sharpening focus, amplifying belief, and accelerating manifestation. The more you engage with these tools, the more effortlessly abundance flows—leading to a life of joy, deeper fulfillment, and expanded possibilities.

Vision Boards: The purpose of vision, or inspirational, boards is to open up the mind to creative ideas that go beyond what we're currently doing in our lives. They come in various types, each tailored to individual preferences, goals, and creative styles. Here are some different types of vision boards and how to create them:

THE TRADITIONAL VISION BOARD (PHYSICAL)

This classic vision board is made with tangible materials like poster boards, magazines, and printed images. To create one, do the following:

- *Gather Materials:* A poster board, scissors, glue, photos, and markers.

- *Arrange the Pieces:* Look for images, quotes, or words that align with the feelings behind your goals and aspirations. Cut them out.

- *Put it Together:* Arrange and glue them onto the board in a way that inspires you.

- *Customize:* Add personal touches like doodles or affirmations written in your handwriting.

Traditional Vision Boards are great for hands-on creatives who enjoy crafting and want a physical reminder to display. Place it somewhere visible so you encounter it daily—on a wall, a closet door, or by your desk.

THE GOAL-SPECIFIC VISION BOARD

This is essentially The Classic Vision Board, but with the focus on a single area of life, such as career, health, relationships, or personal growth. Here's one way to create it:

- *Target In:* Choose one area to focus on (e.g., Fitness Vision Board). Write this at the top or middle of the board, or cut out words to define the board.

- *Gather Materials:* Select images, affirmations, and action steps specific to that area. Remember, baby steps to get there. For example, you might put a photo of someone stretching, then someone swimming, then someone crossing the ribbon on a marathon.

- *Track Your Success:* Include timelines or milestones to track progress visually. For example, if it's fitness, try adding a step counting or miles per month chart.

Goal-Specific Vision Boards are great for people who have a clear, specific goal they want to work on.

THE GRATITUDE VISION BOARD

This variation of The Classic Vision Board focuses on what you're grateful for. Its object is to cultivate an abundance mindset. You can put it together in the following way:

Gather Materials: Find and collect photos, words, or symbols representing the blessings in your life. Some may be actual photos; others may be pictures from a magazine of things like the ocean or trees. You could even have real flowers for your board.

- *Arrange the Pieces:* Put all the elements together on a board alongside quotes and affirmations about gratitude.

The Gratitude Vision Board is perfect if your goal is to focus on positivity and to keep yourself aware of, and living in, the *Attitude of Gratitude.*

THE MIND MAP VISION BOARD

This is essentially The Classic Vision Board, but designed like a mind map with interconnected goals. One approach to accomplishing this is:

- *Create the Core:* Start with a central goal in the middle of your board. For example, it could something simple like a job.

- *Expand Outwardly:* Branch out with sub-goals or supporting actions, using images, symbols, or words for each. In the example above, the job could lead to a bike, which could lead to a car. Or the job could lead to a home or a partner, and maybe a baby. You get the idea.

The Mind Map Vision Board is a way for analytical thinkers who enjoy seeing how goals interconnect to visually represent their goals.

THE DIGITAL VISION BOARD

This is a virtual board created using apps or software. Here's a suggestion how to put it together:

- *Gather Materials:* Collect images, quotes, and designs online that represent your goals.

- *Arrange the Pieces:* Use a design app to arrange them into a collage.

- *Display It:* Set it as your phone or computer wallpaper for daily inspiration, or if its in video style upload it to a digital photo frame and keep it running in a conspicuous place you'll see it often.

Digital Vision Boards are great for tech-savvy individuals or those who prefer an eco-friendly, easily editable option.

THE JOURNAL VISION BOARD

This is a journal, or notebook, based vision board, allowing for portability and ongoing updates. You could try putting it together as follows:

- *Find the Space:* Dedicate a section of your journal for vision board collages. Be sure to leave extra pages in order to expand upon it in the future.
- *Gather Materials:* Add images, affirmations, or sketches that represent your dreams and visions for an abundant life.
- *Allow it to Grow:* Update, revisit and reflect on your entries regularly.

The Manifestation Journal Vision Board works really well for people who enjoy journaling and want a private, portable option. There's an example of, and space for, one of these in *The Perceptual Shift Journal*.

THE VISION BOARD BOX

This interactive, three-dimensional board allows you to place goals and symbols inside a tangible box, adding to it anytime. There are many ways to create the box itself, but for those looking for a simple way to get started, here's an idea:

- *Get a Receptacle:* Find, build or buy a box or basket and fill it with objects, notes, or trinkets representing your dreams.
- *Gather Materials:* Include affirmations, written intentions, or small printed images. Even things like heart-shaped rocks can be fun.
- *Spill It Out:* Once a week dump it all onto a table and look at everything. Make sure that what's in there is still desirable. Add at least on new item.

The Vision Board Box is a fantastic tool to complement your inspiration books and journal, offering a tactile and interactive way to engage with your goals. It allows you to physically connect with your intentions, making the process of manifestation more dynamic and meaningful. It's also a fun way to share your dreams with others, or inspire your kids, friends and partners to create their own.

Putting together and updating vision boards is a powerful practice for focusing and aligning yourself with the gifts of the universe. Remember that abundance is everywhere and it's unlimited. By actively becoming involved in the manifestation process, you open yourself up to more of the good things in life, which everyone deserves.

Scripting: Write a detailed narrative of your ideal life as if it's already happening. Your journal is the perfect place for this exercise, offering a private space to bring your vision to life in words.

To get started, imagine your dream life in vivid detail—where you are, what you're doing, who's with you, and how it feels. Write as though you're already living that reality, using present-tense language. An example for someone wanting a child might be, *"It's amazing to be pregnant, to carry this small child,"* or *"I can't believe I've given birth, my baby is so beautiful."*

Perfection isn't the goal—whether it's a sentence, a paragraph, or a full page, it's already perfect. Leave extra pages in your journal to revisit and expand your script as new ideas or details come to mind. **The goal isn't perfection but capturing the essence of the life you're creating**, setting the stage for it to manifest.

Meditation: Whether you've been meditating all your life or are new to the practice, there are countless ways to incorporate meditation into your journey toward abundance and goal achievement. Meditation is a versatile tool that can help you align your thoughts, emotions, and energy with your intentions, fostering clarity and focus. It can also bring peace, especially when learning to meditate, for example, when in a long line at the store.

For seasoned meditators, or those seeking variety, varied forms of meditation can deepen your practice. Mindfulness meditation centers on being fully present, cultivating awareness and gratitude in each moment. Transcendental meditation uses mantras to transcend thought and achieve deep relaxation, while movement-based practices like yoga or walking meditation combine physical and mental harmony.

For those new to meditation, guided meditations are a great starting point. These structured sessions, often available online or through apps, guide you step-by-step, using visualization, affirmations, and calming techniques to help you relax and connect with your inner self.

Whatever your experience level, choose the style that resonates with you and aligns with your goals. A consistent meditation practice, whether it's five minutes or an hour a day, can help you foster the clarity and focus that helps in manifesting abundance consciousness in your life.

Energy Clearing: Practice techniques like breathwork, sound healing, or yoga in order to release negative energy and align your consciousness with your desires. For those wanting to dive into these areas, here's a few suggestions:

- Clara Harmon's, *The Power of Somatic Therapy* is a highly rated book on breathwork, body awareness and activating the mind-body connection.

- Eileen Day McKusick's book, *Tuning the Human Biofield* is all about using vibrational sound therapy as a form of healing.

- *Yoga for Beginners*, by Cory Martin, is perfect for beginners and those who are looking for simple yoga poses to calm the mind and strengthen the body.

Choose the manifestation method that most excites you—and remember, it's not about the board itself, but the feeling it stirs inside you.

By integrating these advanced techniques into your daily routine, you reinforce your belief in your ability to create abundance and open yourself to the limitless possibilities available to you. Whether through visualization, journaling, or energy clearing, each practice strengthens your alignment with your desires and enhances your capacity to receive.

Remember, manifestation is a dynamic process that thrives on clarity, intention, and consistency. The universe responds to the energy you put out—so focus on what excites, inspires, and fulfills you, and watch as abundance flows into every area of your life.

Do you believe that deepening your manifestation practice with vision boards, scripting, meditation, and energy clearing can strengthen your ability to attract abundance? _____

Choose one advanced manifestation technique from this chapter that resonates with you. Write it down below and explain why it speaks to you.

_____

_____

_____

_____

_____

_____

_____

_____

How do you believe this practice will enhance your ability to manifest abundance? How do you plan to stay consistent in using it? (For example, setting a daily reminder on your phone to practice manifestation for 15 minutes at 10 AM.)

_____

_____

_____

INTEGRATING MANIFESTATION INTO DAILY LIFE

Although we've touched on these throughout this book, here are some quick reminders on how to manifest your desires by consistently practicing simple daily rituals.

Morning Routine: Start your day with rituals that uplift and set a positive tone. The kiss, the wiggle, stretching, yoga, meditation, affirmations, mirror work, shouting "I love my life!" and reading inspirational books are a few I practice daily. It might feel outside your comfort zone at first, but stick with it—your efforts will pay off. For more ideas, revisit *Practical Strategies for Living in the Shift* in the earlier chapter *Living in the Perceptual Shift*.

Mindful Living: Stay present and open to insights and opportunities throughout the day. Approach each moment with curiosity and gratitude, recognizing how your thoughts and actions shape your experiences and relationships. Enhanced awareness allows you to seize opportunities that create abundance, opening doors you might have otherwise overlooked.

Evening Reflection: End your day by reviewing progress and expressing gratitude, perhaps in your journal. Light a candle, meditate, take a relaxing bath, or enjoy herbal tea to unwind. Reflect on the day's victories and lessons, letting go of stress and preparing for restful sleep. Consistent evening rituals are a powerful form of self-care.

Community Support: Share your goals with like-minded individuals who offer encouragement, accountability, and fresh perspectives. Fellowship fosters intimacy—*"into me, you see"*—reminding you that you're not alone on this journey. Supporting and uplifting one another strengthens resilience and multiplies success.

Now it's time to put pencil to paper. Use the following prompts to outline how you'll integrate manifestation into your daily life—not just as a practice, but as a way of being. You'll explore what this looks like in your morning routine, your daily mindset, your evening reflection, and the support systems that will help you stay aligned. Let this be a creative and intentional space to map out the abundant life you're calling forth.

Morning Routine:
What does, or will yours look like?

_____
_____
_____
_____

Mindful Living:
Throughout the day, what will you try to do more often?

_____
_____
_____
_____

Evening Reflection:
What does, or will yours look like?

_____
_____
_____
_____

Community Support:
What groups or fellowship would you like to walk this path with?

_____
_____
_____
_____

INSPIRING STORIES OF MANIFESTATION

The Dream Job: By using manifestation techniques, a woman consistently envisioned herself thriving in her dream industry, envisioning herself feeling the emotions and details as if that were her reality. Motivated by her vision, she began taking purposeful steps, such as networking and pursuing opportunities aligned with her goals. Within a year, her dedication and inspired actions led her to land her ideal role.

The Home of Their Dreams: A couple used vision boards and affirmations to manifest their perfect home. Despite financial challenges, opportunities aligned in ways they never expected, and within six months, they found themselves moving into the house of their dreams. Not every detail was exactly as they had envisioned, but over the years, they've made it even better than they imagined.

Healing and Renewal: A man recovering from illness initially fell into depression, and as research shows, depression can exacerbate physical ailments. Realizing that focusing solely on his challenges was hindering his recovery, he began to shift his mindset—cultivating gratitude for his body's strength and visualizing full health. This transformative change not only accelerated his healing but also inspired him to help others on their own recovery journeys.

Do you relate most to the first, second, or third story? _____

Write why it resonates with you and how it might give you the courage to manifest a desire, even in the face of adversity.

_____

_____

_____

_____

_____

EMBRACING YOUR POWER TO MANIFEST

Manifestation is not magic; it demands deliberate, sustained action to transform intentions into reality. It is a practice of aligning your thoughts, emotions, and actions to create the life you desire. By embracing these principles and practices—and taking purposeful action—you can tap into the transformative power of manifestation to bring your dreams to life.

Remember, manifestation begins within. By cultivating belief in your capabilities, nurturing gratitude, deepening your connection with the source, and coupling these with inspired action, you'll witness your external world transform to reflect your highest aspirations

Take a moment to recognize the abundance already present in your life and the dreams you've manifested so far, knowing that with this mindset, anything is possible. *Your abundant, fulfilling life is within reach—all that's required is to step into it with confidence and intention.*

Do you believe that there are areas of your life today that provide a tremendous amount of abundance? _____

If so, write about the abundance you experience in the following areas of your life:

Abundance in Relationships: *Write down a list of the strong friendships and relationships that provide meaningful and supportive connections in your life. Write a little about how you could expand this even more.*

_____

_____

_____

_____

ABUNDANCE MANIFESTATION PRACTICES

Abundance in Health: *List ways your body supports you daily, whether through strength, energy, or resilience. Write about how you can nurture and appreciate your health even more.*

_____
_____
_____
_____

Abundance in Mindset: *Reflect on your ability to shift perspectives, stay positive, and find opportunities in challenges. Write about a recent time when your mindset helped you navigate a situation successfully.*

_____
_____
_____
_____

Abundance in Career/Purpose: *List the ways your career or daily work provides fulfillment, growth, or financial stability. If you're not fully aligned with your purpose yet, write about steps you can take to get closer to work that inspires you.*

_____
_____
_____
_____

Abundance in Creativity: *Write about how creativity plays a role in your life, whether through art, problem-solving, or innovative thinking. List ways you can invite even more creativity into your daily routine.*

_____
_____
_____
_____
_____

Abundance in Spirituality: *Reflect on the practices or beliefs that bring you peace, meaning, or a sense of connection. Write about how you can deepen this aspect of your life.*

_____
_____
_____
_____
_____

Abundance in Time: *List moments where you truly enjoy how you spend your time. Write about how you can create more space for things that matter most to you.*

_____
_____
_____
_____
_____

ABUNDANCE MANIFESTATION PRACTICES

Abundance in Personal Growth: *Write about key life lessons, moments of transformation, or skills you've developed that have made you wiser and stronger. Consider what area of growth you'd like to focus on next.*

_____
_____
_____
_____

Abundance in Resources: *List the tools, knowledge, and opportunities already available to you. Write about how you can make the most of these resources to create even more abundance.*

_____
_____
_____
_____

Abundance in Simple Joys: *Write about the small daily pleasures that bring happiness into your life—sunsets, music, laughter, pets, or favorite hobbies. Reflect on how you can become even more present in appreciating these moments.*

_____
_____
_____
_____

THE PERCEPTUAL SHIFT

Abundance in Life: *By engaging in this exercise, you not only acknowledge the abundance already present in your life but also set the stage for attracting even more positivity and growth.*

- **Exercise:** *Reflect on the sheer gift of life and the time you've been granted to experience it.*

    ◊ **Calculate Your Age in Seconds:** *Search online for an "Age in Seconds Calculator" to find out exactly how many seconds you've been alive. Write your answer here: _____*

At the time of writing this, **I've had over two billion seconds of this precious gift called life**. Not everyone has been fortunate enough to have this much time to explore, experience, and love.

Now, take a moment to appreciate the abundance of time you've been given. How does it feel to see your life measured in seconds?

_____

_____

Do you now see each moment as more precious? _____

Write a few thoughts about the years, months, weeks, days, hours, minutes, and seconds remaining in your life—and how you can make the most of the time ahead. What would you like to do, experience, or become that you're not yet allowing yourself to?

_____

_____

_____

_____

_____

PUTTING IT ALL TOGETHER
THE ROAD TO TRANSFORMATION

There once was a man named Kavi who lived in a small village surrounded by beauty—but he rarely saw it.

Though he was strong and skilled, Kavi often felt unloved, unseen, and unworthy. His heart was heavy with envy, and his days bitter with disappointment. He hated his life—not because it was unbearable, but because he constantly compared it to the lives he imagined others were living.

He believed the world was against him. But in truth, he had been against the world—closed off, resentful, unwilling to receive the good already around him. The people in his village tried to help, but Kavi never appreciated them. He mistook their kindness as pity, their wisdom as nonsense. What he truly longed for was a life of happiness—content, loved, and fulfilled in every way.

One day, he overheard travelers speaking of a wise old man who lived atop a distant mountain—said to hold the secret to happiness, the key to a fulfilled life. Kavi left the next morning, convinced that if he could only find the old man, he could finally get what he deserved.

He believed the journey would take three days. It took three months.

He was caught in torrential storms.
He fell into a pit so deep he nearly gave up.
He spent days trapped in a tree, surrounded by hyenas.
He went hungry. Got lost. Nearly froze.

To Kavi, these weren't signs. They were setbacks. In his eyes, they only confirmed what he already believed: that life was against him—testing him, punishing him, holding him back.

THE PERCEPTUAL SHIFT

When Kavi finally reached the summit, he was weary, soaked, and aching. An old man sat beside a fire outside a small stone hut. He looked up with clear, knowing eyes and said, *"My son, you look so tired. How long have you been traveling?"*

"Three months," Kavi said, sinking down beside him. And then, slowly, he told the old man everything. When he finished, the old man sat quietly for a moment.

Then he asked, *"Tell me, my son—what is it that you truly want?"*

Kavi thought deeply. Then he said:

"I want three things. First, I want to feel real love—not admiration or approval, but the kind of love that makes life feel worth living.

Second, I want to love my life. I'm tired of feeling restless, bitter, and empty. I want to feel joy in simply being alive.

And third… I want to feel like life is with me, not against me. Like I'm supported, guided—even when things are hard."

The old man nodded gently. *"Then let me ask you something. When the storm came, and the valley turned to a river—how did it feel?"*

"Hopeless," Kavi said. *"I thought I wouldn't survive. I barely found shelter under a narrow ledge. I was soaked and freezing. Then I saw a young deer, stranded on a rock in the water. I didn't want to risk it, but I couldn't watch it drown. I crawled out and pulled it to safety. A few minutes later, the storm broke. The river calmed."*

The old man nodded. *"And how did it feel to save that deer?"*

Kavi looked off for a moment. *"It felt… right. Like I had done something that mattered. It didn't fix everything. But something inside me softened."*

The old man smiled.

"There's your first answer. You asked for love. And you received it the moment you gave it—unselfishly, from the deepest place in your heart, expecting nothing in return. Love is not something you wait for. It's something you become."

"And when you were stuck in the pit," the old man continued, "how did that feel?"

"Like I'd been buried alive," Kavi said. "Initially I was, as dirt and leaves covered my head. I screamed for help. Eventually, a little girl appeared at the edge. She tried to help... but she fell in too."

He paused.

"That's when I really got scared. But there wasn't time to panic. She was crying, and I did what I could to comfort her. I gave her my coat. Held her close. Told her it would be okay. The next morning, there was an earthquake. The rocks shifted. A beam of light came through rocks around us. I managed to move one away and found a narrow passage. Together we climbed out."

The old man nodded. "And how did it feel to escape?"

"I felt... grateful," Kavi said quietly. "Just to be alive."

The old man's expression softened into a knowing smile.

"You asked to love your life. And that was the moment it began. Not because you escaped—but because you remembered life was something worth being grateful for. When you gave comfort to another, and then felt the gift of your own survival—you opened your heart to life itself. You stopped chasing something better, and simply honored what was. And in that moment... you began to truly love being alive."
"And when the hyenas had you trapped in that tree...?"

Kavi sighed. "I felt cursed. Like the universe had me cornered for no reason. I couldn't sleep. Couldn't move. I thought I'd never leave that tree."

"And what happened?"

"There were vines strangling the branches. I pulled at one and noticed tiny suction-like tendrils clinging tightly to the bark. Underneath, I saw deep grooves—marks where the vines had been slowly choking the life from the tree.

Something stirred inside me. I don't know why, but I felt compelled to help. So I began peeling them away. One by one. Slowly. Gently. Day after day. Not because I thought it would change anything… but because it felt like the right thing to do.

And then, one morning, reached for another vine—there were none left. I had removed them all.

I sat there for a moment, my hands resting on the bare branch. I felt… still. Proud that I had completed something that required so much time, diligence, and persistence—without any payment in return. It was a feeling I didn't quite recognize.

Then I realized—I had forgotten about the hyenas. I looked down… and they were gone. I had no idea how long they'd been gone. Maybe hours. Maybe days."

The old man's eyes twinkled.

"You asked to feel supported by life. And life responded. You didn't just wait—you gave care to the very thing that held you up and protected you. And when the tree was finally free, so were you. You supported life—and life supported you back. Do you understand how it works now? You were never abandoned. You were being invited to participate in your own freedom."

He placed a hand gently over Kavi's heart.

"You were not rescued by chance, my son. You were not spared by luck. You were released by love. Every time you gave without asking, every time you *helped without needing reward, the path opened. Not because the world finally gave you what you wanted—but because you became what the world needed. And in doing so, you received what your heart had longed for all along."*

Kavi looked down, silent. The fire cracked. The wind softened. "*I think I understand*," he said quietly. "*But… what do I do now?*" he asked.

The old man smiled.

"*Go home*," he said. "*And do what you did to get here. Care about others. Help them from your heart. Be grateful—like you were when the rain stopped, when the hyenas left, when the earth shifted and light broke through.*

What you experienced on this mountain wasn't just a journey—it was a shift in how you see the world. You stopped asking what life owed you, and started asking what you could offer it.

Live in that awareness. That is the **Perceptual Shift** *that will make all your dreams come true.*"

Kavi returned to his village not as the man who had left—but as someone entirely new. His shoulders no longer carried bitterness. His eyes were softer. His presence calm. Many had assumed he had perished. And in a way, he had. The man who had left was gone. Now, Kavi thanked people. He helped without being asked. The village hadn't changed. But Kavi had.
And now, everywhere he looked—he saw beauty.

And not long after, he saw her.

A woman who had always been there—tending the fields, smiling quietly, living with steady grace. He had passed her a hundred times without truly seeing her. But now… his eyes were open in a different way. They fell in love—not out of longing or fantasy, but out of presence and joy. The love was mutual, rooted, real.

And slowly, the life Kavi had once longed for began arriving. Not because he demanded it, but because he shifted—and let the need for it go. He gave freely. And life gave freely in return.

And truly, he lived happily ever after.

Because the truth is this: Our deepest desires aren't fulfilled by getting more or arriving somewhere. They're fulfilled through the experiences we allow, the love we offer, the gratitude we choose, and the way we show up for the world around us.

That's how we learn to love life. That's how we manifest true abundance.

Have you ever had a shift in perspective that helped you stop chasing—and start appreciating what you already have?" _____

If so, what helped you shift from a mindset of lack to one of gratitude?

_____

_____

_____

_____

_____

This is the *Perceptual Shift*. And now, you're ready to live it. As you reach the conclusion of this book, it's important to pause and reflect on the incredible journey you've undertaken. You've explored the profound impact of perception on your life, embraced change, taken steps to cultivate gratitude, and learned to harness the art of manifestation. All of this is leading to increased abundance. Guaranteed.

Each chapter has equipped you with tools and insights to transform your life, and align with your highest potential. Now, it's time to bring it all together into a cohesive plan for living in *The Perceptual Shift* every day.

KEY LESSONS FROM THE JOURNEY

Let's revisit the most important lessons from each chapter and explore how they interconnect to create a life of joy, abundance, and authenticity. Try each key action in this section, and check it off once completed.

The Power of Perception: Your lens shapes your reality. Changing how you view yourself, others, and the world opens the door to infinite possibilities and unlocks your potential for growth, connection, and change.

◊ **KEY ACTION** > Becoming aware of your perceptions is the first step toward transformation. Acknowledge that this awareness has already begun to shift your mindset and open your heart to greater abundance, laying a foundation for meaningful change. Close your eyes, take a deep breath, and feel proud of yourself.

Check this box once completed: ☐

The Inherited Belief System: Family, culture, and past experiences influence your perceptions. Recognizing and challenging these internalized opinions and attitudes allows you to craft a healthier, more empowering narrative that better aligns with your true self.

◊ **KEY ACTION** > Reflect on the origins of your beliefs and consciously choose those that empower you. This intentional process strengthens your sense of self and gives you the confidence to create a life aligned with your values and aspirations. Close your eyes, breathe deeply, and let go of all past experiences that influenced you negatively—acknowledging that although you've learned from them, it's now time to release them.

Check this box once completed: ☐

Becoming More Aware: Moments of awareness often spark transformation, and expanding that awareness turns everything into an opportunity. As we expand our awareness, *Perceptual Shifting* becomes second nature, paving the way for greater abundance, happiness, and peace in your life.

◊ **KEY ACTION** > Close your eyes and breathe deeply. Notice how your perceptions have already begun to shift since you started opening yourself up to—and practicing—the insights shared in this book.

Check this box once completed: ☐

The Art of Reframing: Viewing challenges as opportunities offers a fresh perspective. Small shifts in attitude reveal potential, transforming setbacks into catalysts for growth. The more you practice reframing, the easier it becomes.

◊ **KEY ACTION** > Take a calming breath and pause. Think of a recent challenge that turned into an opportunity. Now, consider a current unresolved obstacle and visualize it transforming into an opportunity. Notice how simply imagining the possibility of resolution can open the door to uncovering the hidden opportunity for growth within.

Check this box once completed: ☐

Welcoming Change: Nothing stays stagnant—change is inevitable and often necessary for growth. Embracing it with courage and flexibility allows you to evolve and thrive. Don't just accept change—welcome it wholeheartedly. Each challenge is an opportunity to learn, adapt, and unlock untapped potential, creating personal transformation and resilience. View change as an ally, not an enemy.

◊ **KEY ACTION** > Gently close your eyes and return to your breath. Reflect on the changes in your life—the moments you resisted and the times you embraced them—and see how wonderfully it all turned out. Now, resolve to choose the softer, easier path of making peace with change, trusting that the universe always has your best interests at heart.

Check this box once completed: ☐

LIVING IN THE PERCEPTUAL SHIFT

Gratitude as a Compass: Gratitude shifts your focus from lack to abundance, fostering joy and attracting positive energy. An attitude of gratitude is the result of daily, conscious effort. By practicing gratitude every day—even when things aren't going your way—you master the art of *Perceptual Shifting*.

◊ **KEY ACTION** > Let your eyelids fall and draw air into your lungs, fully and calmly. Bring to mind one moment, one event, or one accomplishment you're most grateful for in your life. Let that feeling of abundance remind you that gratitude is a daily, conscious practice— not only for celebrating the wonderful but also for transforming even the toughest challenges into opportunities for joy and growth when you live in an *Attitude of Gratitude*.

Check this box once completed: ☐

Perceptual Shifting in Relationships: Healthy relationships enrich our lives by providing support and growth, and when we approach them with empathy, curiosity, and an open heart, they foster deeper understanding and connection.

◊ **KEY ACTION** > Soften your gaze, close your eyes, and inhale deeply. Visualize someone in your life with whom you share a great relationship—how does it feel to love them and be loved by them? Now, think of a challenging relationship and imagine it transformed into one that is just as loving and kind. If it's difficult, that's understandable. But this act of visualization is a *Perceptual Shift* with the power to manifest your deepest desires. It may not happen immediately, but keep at it and watch as subtle shifts in your life begin to unfold.

Check this box once completed: ☐

Creating a New Roadmap: Directional blueprints, aligned with your values and aspirations, provide clarity and empower you to take purposeful action—reinforcing the *Perceptual Shifts* that keep you aligned with your goals. Set clear objectives and take consistent steps toward your vision.

THE PERCEPTUAL SHIFT

◊ **KEY ACTION** > Create a visualization tool, like a vision board or goal journal. While it takes effort, it helps you see your desired future, stay focused, and align daily actions with your aspirations—bringing more of the abundance you deserve into your life.

Check this box once completed: ☐

Living in the Shift: *The Perceptual Shift* is the art of recognizing the beauty, opportunity, and wisdom hidden in every moment. By understanding that perception shapes reality, you can consciously choose to shift. Pause. Reframe challenges. Move toward positivity. Over time, this becomes second nature—a gentle reflex that transforms your entire experience of life.

◊ **KEY ACTION** > Settle into stillness—eyes closed, breath deep. Recall a recent uncomfortable interaction. Replay it, but this time, imagine releasing resistance to the other person's words or actions. Welcome the moment as a chance to shift your perception.

Take it further: picture them as a child—still learning, still growing, sometimes struggling. Feel compassion for them, and gratitude for your own release of old patterns like reacting, defending, or blaming.

This is *Perceptual Shifting*. Practice it throughout your day—especially whenever you feel out of alignment or in a state of "dis-ease."

Check this box once completed: ☐

Your Abundant Life Awaits: Abundance is a mindset. By focusing on gratitude, possibility, and generosity, you create a life beyond your wildest dreams. It starts within and radiates outward. When you notice a mindset of lack, consciously shift to gratitude and the opportunities around you. This awareness, paired with action, is the essence of *The Perceptual Shift*.

◊ **KEY ACTION** > Turn inward—close your eyes and breathe with intention. Imagine your life overflowing with love, opportunities, and joy. Feel the security and gratitude of knowing you are always supported. Now, think of one area where you've been stuck in lack. Reframe it—what blessings already exist? What's one small step toward abundance? Hold onto this feeling and carry it with you throughout the day, allowing it to flow naturally.

Check this box once completed: ☐

Manifestation Practices: By harmonizing your intentions, emotions, and actions, you activate the flow of abundance. Manifestation is an intentional collaboration with the infinite intelligence of the universe. Clarity, belief, and action are the pillars of manifestation.

- ◊ **KEY ACTION** > Integration is the key to lasting transformation and successful manifestation. Incorporate the actions, habits, and tools from this book into your daily life. Start small and build gradually until your daily routine is overflowing with gratitude, awareness, and intentional action—naturally aligning you with abundance.

Check this box once completed: ☐

Consistency and mindfulness help you stay aligned with your values, empowering you to navigate challenges with resilience and optimism. There will be tough days, but perfection isn't the goal—realignment is. Keep shifting back to gratitude, growth, and abundance, trusting that even setbacks are part of your journey forward

After going through this book, do you feel more optimistic and like life is becoming lighter and easier? _____

If so, write down which areas of your life have improved and describe how your mindset and approach to life have changed.

_____

_____

_____

BRINGING IT TO LIFE

Now that you have the tools and insights to live in *The Perceptual Shift*, how can you apply them in a cohesive and sustainable way? Here's a blueprint for your path forward:

Start with Awareness: Begin each day with mindfulness. Take a moment to reflect on your perceptions and set an intention to approach the day with an open mind and heart. Create morning rituals that cultivate love, happiness, and appreciation for life. *Write down which morning rituals you'd like to incorporate to support your desire to love life and create abundance.*

_____

_____

_____

Practice Daily Gratitude: Regularly write down what you're grateful for each morning or evening. Use landmarks, bridges, or signs you pass regularly as reminders to say something you're grateful for out loud. Let gratitude shape your mindset, keeping you focused on abundance and positivity throughout the day. *Write down a few things you're grateful for right this moment.*

_____

_____

_____

Reframe Challenges: When faced with obstacles, ask yourself: *How can I see this differently? What's the opportunity here?* Shift back into gratitude as quickly as possible and look for the growth within each experience. *What's one example of something you've recently reframed in a positive way?*

_____

_____

_____

Set Intentions and Goals: Create a roadmap for your dreams and revisit it regularly. Make sure your goals align with your values, and adjust them as needed. Enjoy the process—anything is possible when you stay open to abundance. *What are a few goals, dreams, and desires you'd like to manifest in your life?*

_____

_____

_____

_____

Cultivate Compassion in Relationships: Listen actively and seek to understand others' perspectives. Approach conflicts as opportunities for growth and deeper connection. When needed, detach with love and return with an open heart and mind. *Who are some people you'd like to strengthen your relationships with?*

_____

_____

_____

Embrace Transitions: Change is constant. Flexibility and adaptability help you navigate life's shifts with ease. Trust that every detour has meaning and purpose, leading you toward something greater. *What is one change in your life that you initially saw as negative but later was grateful for?*

_____

_____

_____

Manifest Your Vision: Use visualization, affirmations, and inspired action to bring your dreams to life. Trust the manifestation process, and celebrate your progress, growth, and achievements along the way. *What are three things you'd like to visualize daily to enhance your life?*

_____

_____

_____

Learn from setbacks, build on successes, and recommit to the possibility that every situation and interaction is an opportunity for abundance. By shifting your perception, you transform your reality.

Living in *The Perceptual Shift* is not a one-time event but an ongoing, intentional practice. As mentioned earlier—and reiterated in the introduction to this book—repetition is essential for establishing a strong, healthier foundation.

Surround yourself with like-minded individuals who uplift and inspire you. Share your journey with them, and stay open to learning and growth. *Perceptual Shifting* is an ongoing process—it's natural to forget at times. The key is awareness; when you notice you've drifted, simply realign with joy and abundance. Celebrate your progress, no matter how small, and write it down to reinforce positive habits. Be kind to yourself, trust the journey, and remember—it's a marathon, not a sprint.

You've reached the end of the final chapter of this book—an incredible milestone in your journey toward greater awareness, abundance, and joy. But the real transformation begins now, as you take what you've learned and put it into practice each day.

After reading this book and doing these exercises, do you feel it has helped you love life a little more and encouraged you to believe that you have some power to manifest your dreams? _____

If so, what specific changes have you noticed in your mindset, emotions, or daily experiences since you began this work?

_____
_____
_____
_____
_____

What's one area of your life where you'd like to be even more consistent in applying the principles of The **Perceptual Shift***?*

_____
_____
_____
_____
_____

What is one affirmation or mantra you'll use to remind yourself to live in **The Perceptual Shift** *every day?*

_____
_____
_____
_____
_____

THE PERCEPTUAL SHIFT

What practical steps will you take to hold yourself accountable for maintaining this shift? Will you journal, set reminders, or find an accountability partner?

_____
_____
_____
_____
_____

If you could share one powerful lesson from this book with someone you care about, what would it be?

_____
_____
_____
_____
_____

If you could gift this book to one person and encourage them to do the work, who would it be and why?

_____
_____
_____
_____
_____

A FINAL REFLECTION

Reaching this point in the book is no small feat—**congratulations**! Few people take the time to reflect, grow, and intentionally create a life they love. Your commitment to this journey speaks to both your courage and your dedication to transformation.

Now, if you haven't already, it's time to begin practicing these principles each day.

By embracing *The Perceptual Shift*, you've taken a bold step toward living more authentically, joyfully, and abundantly. As you apply these tools, you may find yourself—like me—joyfully proclaiming, "*I love my life!*" every day.

Your path is uniquely yours, and its possibilities are limitless. Step forward with confidence, gratitude, and the belief that the best is yet to come. As you continue to evolve, you'll naturally inspire others to explore their own growth and potential—encouraging them to shift as well.

Writing this book has been an honor—a dream over 20 years in the making. My hope is that the ideas and stories shared here have touched your heart, shifted your perspective, and made a meaningful difference in your life.

If you'd like to share your thoughts or experiences, I'd love to hear from you. Feel free to reach out at theperceptualshift@gmail.com—your feedback is always welcome.

Thank you for joining me on this incredible adventure of self-discovery and transformation. May your life be filled with love, joy, abundance, and the beauty of your own *Perceptual Shift*.

With deep gratitude,

James Quine, Life Lover

DAILY PRACTICES OF LIFE LOVERS
ESSENTIAL ROUTINES TO FOSTER ABUNDANCE

Loving life is not a passive state—it's an intentional, daily practice. I've been a confirmed, dedicated, and adamant life lover since 2003. Though I likely came into this world as one, life events pulled me off track for decades. I spent years merely tolerating life—or outright disliking it. Everything changed when I made a conscious decision to love life again.

But let me be clear: I'm far from perfect at this.

These habits I'm about to share? They're ones I strive to follow—but rarely all in a single day. Some days, I practice most of them. Other days, I barely touch one. And yes, there are times I completely fall off track. But the difference in my attitude, my outlook, how I treat others (and how I'm treated), and the abundance I notice and receive—those shifts are a direct reflection of how consistently I return to these practices.

When I fail, I sometimes fail hard. But when I succeed... the results are nothing short of miraculous. And most of all, when I stay connected to these rituals, something beautiful happens: I believe not only in myself—but in the sweetness of life.

So if you find yourself stumbling, that's okay. Me too. What matters is that you keep coming back. These daily practices aren't about perfection. They're about direction. They're here to help you shift—back into love, into gratitude, into the fullness of life.

You'll find these practices outlined on the pages that follow. As always, take what resonates—and leave the rest.

MORNING RITUALS & INTENTIONS

- ☐ **Wake Up with Gratitude**: Before opening your eyes, kiss your fingers and lift them to the sky in gratitude. You've been given the gift of another day.

- ☐ **Appreciate Your Body**: Wiggle your fingers and toes. Stretch gently, even before getting out of bed. Feel thankful for the movement and function of your body.

- ☐ **Celebrate Your Senses**: As you open your eyes, acknowledge the miracle of sight, hearing, touch—whatever gifts are available to you today.

- ☐ **Speak Loving Words**: Look into your eyes in the mirror and say, "I love you." Kiss a photo of your younger self and promise to bring joy and fun into the day.

- ☐ **Welcome Abundance**: Raise your arms to the sky and speak this aloud: *"I open myself to abundance—in love, finances, health, creativity, kindness, and whatever else the universe has in store. Bring it in!"*

- ☐ **Set an Intention**: Choose one word or phrase that represents how you want to feel or show up today (e.g., "present," "grateful," "open to joy").

- ☐ **Affirm Your Power**: Say aloud: "I love my life!"—whether you fully feel it or not. Energy follows focus.

- ☐ **Read or Listen to Something Uplifting**: Feed your mind and soul before consuming anything stressful.

- ☐ **Do a Morning Yogatation**: Meditate and move your body.

DAILY PRACTICE OF LIFE LOVERS

THROUGHOUT THE DAY

- ☐ **Live in the Attitude of Gratitude**: Keep a running list of things you're grateful for. If you're stuck, list a body part, a favorite food, or something beautiful you saw today.

- ☐ **Stay Calm Under Pressure**: When agitated, pause. Breathe. Then respond rather than react.

- ☐ **Practice Presence**: Bring joy into mundane moments. Watch your breath, feel your feet, notice beauty.

- ☐ **Nourish Your Body**: Eat well, move daily, hydrate, and rest. Balance treats with care.

- ☐ **Make Time for Fun**: Joy is essential. When bored, it's your inner child asking for playtime.

- ☐ **Release the Need to Be Right**: Remain open to the possibility that others have something valuable to share.

- ☐ **Stay Out of the Drama**: If energy feels toxic, excuse yourself, take a walk, or create space.

- ☐ **Recognize Victim Thinking**: Catch yourself when blaming, complaining, or throwing a "pity party." Shift to empowerment.

- ☐ **Take Responsibility**: When you mess up, own it. Make amends. Then recommit to being your best self.

- ☐ **Trust the Process**: Don't force it. Breathe. Relax. Answers will come.

- ☐ **Stay in Your Hula Hoop**: Focus on your own growth, joy, and perspective—let others live their own lives.

EVENING REFLECTION & WINDING DOWN

- ☐ **Review the Day with Kindness**: Journal your wins, reflect on any slip-ups, and learn from both.

- ☐ **Connect with Others**: Engage with people who lift you up. If possible, share your wins and gratitude aloud.

- ☐ **Unplug Early**: Disconnect from screens at least 30 minutes before bed.

- ☐ **Create a Bedtime Ritual**: Light a candle, take a bath, sip tea, or meditate to soothe your body and mind.
- ☐ **Give Thanks One Last Time**: Before you close your eyes, whisper a final thank you for the gift of this day.

- ☐ **Forgive Yourself**: If you fell short of your intentions, be gentle. Celebrate your progress and know tomorrow is a new chance.

WHY THIS WORKS

These habits aren't about perfection—they're about consistency and care. The more often you practice them, the more your neural pathways shift toward joy, gratitude, and abundance. You won't love life every second, but you'll begin to love it more often, more deeply, and more freely.

This is the essence of Living in the *Perceptual Shift*.

GREAT BOOKS TO EXPAND YOUR JOURNEY
RECOMMENDED READING

My experience, strength, and hope have been shaped by many influences throughout my life. Below are some books and authors that have had a profound impact—helping me love my life, find peace, and create an ever-expanding world of abundance.

These titles have touched me deeply, and I hope they inspire and uplift you as well. Let your curiosity guide you—each book you discover is another step toward greater awareness, emotional growth, and joyful living.

- A Deep Breath of Life – Alan Cohen
- A New Earth – Eckhart Tolle
- Attitudes of Gratitude in Love – M.J. Ryan
- Drop the Rock – Bill P.
- Miracle of Mindfulness – Thích Nhất Hạnh
- The Daily Stoic – Ryan Holiday
- The Language of Letting Go – Melody Beattie
- The Power of Now – Eckhart Tolle
- Until Today – Iyanla Vanzant
- You Can't Make Me Angry – Dr. Paul O.

Feel free to explore beyond this list—each book you read is another step toward greater self-awareness, joy, and abundance, while also expanding your emotional intelligence. Let your curiosity guide you, and keep expanding your journey!

CREATING A CIRCLE OF LOVE
SUPPORT AND SERVICE

While personal reflection is a cornerstone of this journey, the process becomes even more powerful when shared with others. Consider using this book in a group setting, where you and your peers can support and uplift one another. Sharing experiences, challenges, and victories creates a sense of fellowship that fosters deeper growth.

Committing to regular meetups can serve as a powerful motivator, encouraging consistent steps toward shifting perception and cultivating abundance. In group discussions, each person can:

- *Take turns reading from inspirational literature like this book.*
- *Share insights and lessons learned from each chapter.*
- *Reflect on journaling experiences and perspective-shifting breakthroughs.*
- *Encourage and celebrate each other's growth.*

The collective energy and shared wisdom of a group can be incredibly inspiring and affirming. Whether you gather with friends, a support group, or a book club, this collaborative approach adds a rich layer of connection, accountability, and momentum to your personal transformation.

Do you have a circle of friends, family, or peers who might be interested in going through this book together as a way to support each other and deepen the experience. _____

If so, write down the group members, day of the week and time you'll meet, and location (in-person, online, etc.). This will help you stay accountable and create a supportive environment as you move through the book together.

Group Members: _____

Weekly Meeting Day: _____ *Weekly Meeting Time* _____

Weekly Meeting Location: _____

www.ingramcontent.com/pod-product-compliance
Lightning Source LLC
Chambersburg PA
CBHW051939290426
44110CB00015B/2044